The New Zealand
Deer Hunter's Handbook
and Resource Guide

DEDICATION

To a new generation of young hunters who face new challenges. I hope this book will encourage and equip you to become safe and successful hunters.

ACKNOWLEDGEMENTS

I'd like to express my thanks to all those who contributed to this book in one way or another, whether by contributing short articles or photos or valued input. I've given acknowledgement where appropriate.

Special thanks also to Graham Gurr, my publisher from The Halcyon Press, whose insights, comments and encouragement have been immensely valued in the publication of my three books. Finally, I'd like to thank my wife Ros, who is an extremely good editor, though not a passionate hunter herself, for the hours spent assisting me.

The New Zealand Deer Hunter's Handbook
and Resource Guide

Alex M. Gale

Published by
The Halcyon Press.
A division of
Halcyon Publishing Ltd.
P.O. Box 360, Auckland 1140, New Zealand.

Printed by
Prolong Press Ltd
China

No part of this publication may be reproduced, stored in a retrieval system or transmitted in any form or by any means, electronic, mechanical, photocopy, recording or otherwise without prior written permission of the publisher.

ISBN 978-1-877256-60-8
Copyright © Alex Gale 2006, 2008
First Published 2006
Reprinted 2008, 2011
All Rights Reserved

Cover photo: Grateful thanks to Nathan McClunie for the use of this photo.

By the same author:
Hunting for Love and For Money
They Don't Come Easy

www.halcyonpublishing.co.nz

CONTENTS

Preface   7

Introduction   8

Part One

PREPARATION FOR THE HUNT

1	New Zealand Deer Species	11
2	Gear	23
3	Personal preparation	32
4	Five tips from a gunsmith to improve the accuracy of your rifle	37
5	Tips on knives	45
6	To hunt and return — developing safe hunting practice	49
7	From the Hunting Doctor	52
8	When you get lost!	68

Part Two

FROM THE KILL TO THE CARRY

9	Stalking tips	73
10	Shoot to kill	77
11	Field butchery and hygiene issues	79
12	How to carry out a deer whole	86
13	In camp	98
14	Keeping your skins	99
15	If you shoot a trophy	101

Part Three

PREPARING YOUR MEAT

16	Cutting it up yourself	107

17	What your butcher wants	117
18	A new world of options	118
19	Storage	120

Part Four

ENJOY! RECIPES AND TIPS

20	Venison recipes, compliments of Deer Industry New Zealand	123
21	Venison recipes - General	134
22	Venison jerky (Homemade)	137
23	Recommended books	138

Addendum

I	Butchers who specialise in quality venison products	141
II	Websites of interest	142
III	Backcountry transport and charter operators	148
IV	Taxidermists	153
V	Gunsmiths	156
VI	A warning	159
VII	Review of non-commercial wild food in New Zealand (excerpts)	162
VIII	Final Comments	168

PREFACE

A GLORIOUS PAST, A GREAT FUTURE…

Back in the '60s when I started hunting, we shot deer with cut-down army surplus .303s and ex-military ammunition, left the carcasses to rot, sold the tails to the Chinese and picked up three .303 rounds for the ears from the Government. That was also the era when you could sell kea beaks for a bounty! Times have definitely changed!

Then came the meat hunting era when people made more from a day's shooting than from a week's pay, followed by the exciting live capture days when deer were living gold and worth more alive than dead. Today feral deer are relatively worthless except for their recreational value and it is time to re-evaluate the whole hunting scene. Rather than selling animals, hunters are now looking at other ways of utilising their valued game. There's a new world out there in terms of what hunters can do with their meat, rather than using it as a means to increase the income.

We'll explore some of these options and show you all the aspects of butchery a hunter needs to know, particularly with regard to deer but, more than that, we'll also outline certain factors that lead to a successful hunt and a good outcome in terms of the products.

You'll be surprised at what you can do with your valued game meat.

I'm very aware as I write this that other experienced hunters may see things from another perspective and will do some things differently. We all have our own preferences and that's fine. How boring if we all thought the same. We never stop learning. In fact this book has evolved as it has been written and it's been another learning curve. No doubt I'll miss some things out that others regard as important — that is inevitable, but I trust this book will be of assistance to many as they enjoy the wonderful experience of hunting in New Zealand.

Alex Gale December 2007

INTRODUCTION

"Eternal life is the ultimate trophy. Make that your aim, but enjoy to the max God's creation. May all your trips be good ones. Good hunting and straight shooting." This was the inscription Dad wrote inside my copy of his first book, *Hunting for Love and for Money*.

Over the years people have always told me how lucky I've been to be brought up by a skilled hunter and outdoorsman, and for the most part I've taken this gift for granted. As time goes on I realise what a privilege I've been given and I've learnt to make the most of what I've been taught.

Had it not been for my dad I would never have learnt such a great love for the bush, the mountains, the times away with good companions, the memories you make and, of course, the animals you hunt. I wouldn't have learnt all those things which have become second nature like keeping the wind in your face, where to look for deer, how to stalk them, right through to the final processes of the hunt. These are just a few of the things I've learnt from him.

Dad has not just been an invaluable teacher, but also a great father to look up to, and as I've got older he has also become one of my best friends. As you read through *The New Zealand Deer Hunter's Handbook* I hope you take away some hard-earned knowledge from a hunter with over 40 years' experience so that you too can be more successful and have a more enjoyable time in our great outdoors. I wish him great success and happiness in all he does.

Tim Gale

December 2005

PART ONE

PREPARATION FOR THE HUNT

- New Zealand Deer Species
- Gear
- Personal preparation
- Five tips from a gunsmith to improve the accuracy of your rifle
- Tips on knives
- To hunt and return — developing safe hunting practice
- From the "Hunting Doctor"
- When you get lost!

A thinking hunter is a safe and successful hunter.

Chapter 1   NEW ZEALAND DEER SPECIES

In this brief overview I have deliberately omitted Wapiti and Moose. If you find one of the latter, your name will be forever engraved in the annals of New Zealand hunting history. Even if you find one of yesterday's droppings it will probably be regarded as a trophy of some sort! Quite easy to mount too. The Wapiti in Fiordland aren't much better. At best today you will get a nice hybrid which is unfortunate, as they are a magnificent game animal whose demise is a testimony to ignorance, greed, stupidity and gross mismanagement!

RED DEER

Red deer are New Zealand's most popular and enduring big game animal. Widespread in both South and North Islands as well as in Stewart Island, Red deer were first released here in 1851. Although that release was unsuccessful,

Two Red deer hinds. Can you spot the fawn?

further deer imported from England, Scotland and Australia and released in a number of places ensured that they became successfully established.

They have adapted incredibly well to New Zealand conditions, including high hunting pressure, and are found in high tussock country and down to heavily forested lowland beech forest. Weights of Red deer vary according to breeding, area, population density and available feed. In some areas a stag of 110kg would be large while in other areas they may reach 230kgs. An average hind would probably weigh in at less than 70kg.

The high point of the hunting year for most New Zealand hunters coincides with the Red deer roar, beginning as early as mid March in some areas, but usually about the second week in April, and lasting in varying intensity for two to three weeks, although I have heard Red stags roar as late as the end of May. Apart from the roar, good times to hunt Red deer are in May, as the stags are feeding up large for the winter, and in the spring when there is new growth around. Red deer are more forgiving to hunt than, say, Sika: they seem more placid in nature and not so toey, which is probably one reason most people hunt them. In the spring, when the hinds kick off their yearlings, it is often not difficult to get a shot at these young animals — stupidity and inquisitiveness mean a good number find their way into freezers each year.

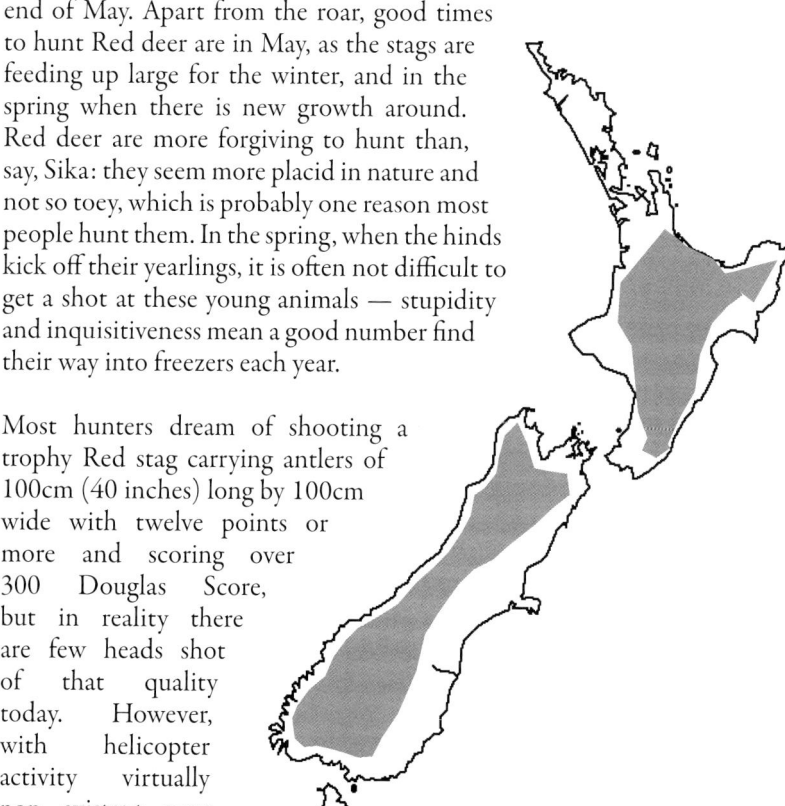

Most hunters dream of shooting a trophy Red stag carrying antlers of 100cm (40 inches) long by 100cm wide with twelve points or more and scoring over 300 Douglas Score, but in reality there are few heads shot of that quality today. However, with helicopter activity virtually non existent now and hunters exercising better judgement and discipline in leaving young potential trophies to grow and mature, the future looks good.

FALLOW DEER

New Zealand hunters have an interesting attitude to Fallow deer, seeing them as a poor cousin to Reds or even Sika. In fact many North Island hunters seem to look down their noses at them — they obviously haven't hunted Fallow deer in the Blue Mountains of Otago where they seem to have acquired completely different characteristics to their blood brothers in the North Island herd. After hunting both Sika and Blue Mountains Fallow extensively I'd say that there was little difference in their relative hunting difficulty.

Fallow deer were introduced into New Zealand in 1864 and there are now at least nine well known and established herds in both the South and North Islands, plus numerous small private herds in many areas in both islands. Here enterprising hunters and/or owners have exercised their vision for the future in the face of DoC's extermination policy. I can understand their rationale. The best known herds are in the Wanganui area, the Blue Mountains of Otago and the Lake Wakatipu area.

Apart from having a palmated antler structure, the most unusual feature of Fallow deer is their colouring, which ranges from white to a chestnut ginger with white spots to a black/grey. I have only ever seen three white ones. Note that they are not an albino, but a true white. Fallow are significantly smaller than Red deer, but some bucks will weigh in at over 95kg. Nice venison too.

The rutting season begins in late April, but I have heard them in a full blown roar in late March in the Wanganui area. A Fallow buck certainly doesn't sound like a Red — it is more of a hormonally charged cross between a croak and a grunt.

If you can shoot a Fallow buck that scores over 200 Douglas score you will have a fantastic trophy. I scored one last year that went 254 — it looked like a small moose. Unfortunately I didn't shoot it. While many of the huge Fallow heads appearing nowadays are coming from these private liberations, there is a good future for Fallow and a better one for North Island hunters if we can cull out of the Wanganui herd the breeding that produces split palms, and introduce some quality stags to the herd. Proper game management in New Zealand is probably an oxymoron, but it shouldn't be so.

Finally, if Fallow have one fatal flaw it is probably this — they are creatures of habit more so than Reds. They tend to stick to the same areas and in that respect are quite predictable, but don't quote me on that when you try for a trophy buck!

SIKA DEER

I love hunting Sika, especially in the roar. They are vocal, they are cheeky, they are aggressive and they are a challenge. No doubt about it, they are the premiere species of the North Island. Just observe the huge number of vehicles in the car parks of various helicopter operators during the roar in April and you will have some idea of the number of hopefuls who venture into the hills at this time. Few return though with more than a handful of photos, good stories, lightened wallets and hope of better luck for the next year.

Sika are an attractive animal about the size of Fallow deer, first released successfully at Poronui Station near Taupo in 1905. Since then they have aggressively colonised the Kaimanawa, Ahimanawa and Kaweka Ranges, successfully pushing out the Red deer, and are also found in the west Whirinaki, around the east side of Tongariro and even to the north end of the Tararuas in small numbers.

Sika are the most vocal of all deer species in New Zealand: they will play

Fallow deer does.

hide and seek with a noisy hunter, squealing loudly while hiding, while the stags will loudly herald the event of a hind coming into season, surely an example of the masculine ego gone wild! For that reason, it is sometimes possible to call them in. Having told all and sundry that a bit of action is at hand, they then feel it is their duty to give all consequent intruders short shrift, an unfortunate action that often results in the number two stag being left to do the job the number one chap had lined up! A good if rather permanent example of acting in haste and repenting at leisure.

March is a good time to begin your search for a top Sika trophy. Stags will often be found right out in the open, sometimes long distances from the bush. Take a good pair of binoculars, park yourself on a good vantage point and you may be surprised at what you see. The best way to bush hunt Sika in the roar is either to sit on the edge

Sika deer.

of a feed area right on dawn or dusk and wait, or if bush hunting, to roar in response to a stag's roar, get yourself into a good position and wait, or roar and wait when finding a fresh pad. And by wait I mean for a lot more time than it takes to look down and count your feet. Don't then shoot the first stag that appears — he may be the Sika counterpart of a hormone charged teenager, when what you are looking for is your counterpart: a big, strong, mature and impressive looking record book male. Look at the top of the antlers if you can while the buck fever is setting in to see if he has two points on top, so ensuring he is at least an eight pointer. Winter time is one of the best times to obtain a good Sika head. There are few hunters around and stags often out feeding. We have shot more 8 point Sika stags after the end of April than at any other time.

A top Sika head is an impressive trophy and will have eight points to score over 170 Douglas score. Not too many like that are shot each year, going by entries in the annual Sika contest in Taupo and given the number of hunters targeting Sika. Good luck.

Red stag and hinds in the tussock. (Photo: Simon Gibson)

Red deer are the most popular deer species in New Zealand and probably the easiest to hunt. This hind is wondering what this strange creature is on about!

Lots of good meat here with these two Red deer. The yearling on the left would make very good eating. Looks like she is waiting to be invited into the freezer! An easy neck shot would do the trick!

The magic of hunting is in the unexpected. There is a special beauty in nature only experienced at dawn and dusk.

RUSA DEER

Only a small handful of dedicated hunters target Rusa deer. Most hunters don't seem to have the necessary skills or patience to succeed with them, and for good reason: they're probably the most difficult species in New Zealand to hunt.

Released near Galatea at the foot of the Urewera Ranges in 1908, they were initially thought to be Sambar and were not correctly identified until 1955 as being Rusa. You see it is not only politicians who fail to see the obvious. Rusa have now spread along the western side of the Urewera Forest Park and

Rusa deer, Urewera National Park. (Photo: Dave Barraclough)

back east of the Whakatane River, being found mainly in small pockets. You won't see many.

A mature stag will weigh in at around 100 kg plus and will sport a six point antler structure. Rusa look unmistakably different to a Red deer, having a more chocolate colour, a whitish underside and a longer tail. Their rut begins mid July and is a predominantly quiet affair, for the hunter that is. The stags may think otherwise. Rusa seldom roar and, if so, it's usually at night. Those who have been fortunate to have heard their roar describe it as being like a calf bellow. Rusa are certainly not as aggressive in their roaring as, say, a Sika, and I know of no hunter who has called them in by imitating their roar. You can try bush hunting them, but believe you me this is a very difficult and often fruitless occupation guaranteed to promote frustration, if not premature insanity. Probably the best hunting technique is to find an area Rusa inhabit, and from an observation point looking out over a clearing facing north or a semi open north face, sit and watch. You will be sitting in the freezing cold more often than not while the Rusa will be looking for the sunny spots as they seem to love steep semi open faces and early morning sunlight. Not a bad trade off I suppose, as after all at the end of the day you will still have your life while hopefully a trophy stag will have met his demise. Well that's the theory we eternally optimistic hunters subscribe to. Take a good book, effective binoculars, plenty of patience and look up often — one minute there will be nothing, the next a Rusa will have ghosted onto the clearing. And it might be a stag! Apart from July and August, a profitable and definitely warmer time to target a Rusa stag is in the spring as they don't cast their antlers until about late December. Be prepared for a long shot. And make sure you can shoot straight.

If you get a six point Rusa with antlers over 75cm (30 inches) in length, you will be a very fortunate hunter indeed and probably will have hunted long and hard. They do make a magnificent trophy though. A final comment — hunt and shoot with an eye to the future: if you see an immature stag, please let it go. They don't grow bigger by shooting them. It's your future — maybe next time!

WHITETAIL

If deer could enter a beauty contest, surely the whitetail would win. If you've ever seen the long white flashing tail and rump disappearing in a graceful

Whitetail does. (Photo: John DeLury)

leap through the fern, you'll know what I mean. Released in New Zealand in 1905, Whitetail have found a home on Stewart Island and at the head of Lake Wakatipu. They have a kind of fragile look and weigh slightly less than a Fallow deer, but there the similarity ends. Their antler structure is quite different to other deer in New Zealand: Whitetail antlers rise vertically and then curve forward. Unfortunately here they don't seem to grow the same eye-catching heads as found in the USA or Canada. Not sure why — must be the beer we drink, I reckon. The heads do seem to be getting better though and in fact any head with 8 or more points is generally considered a trophy here.

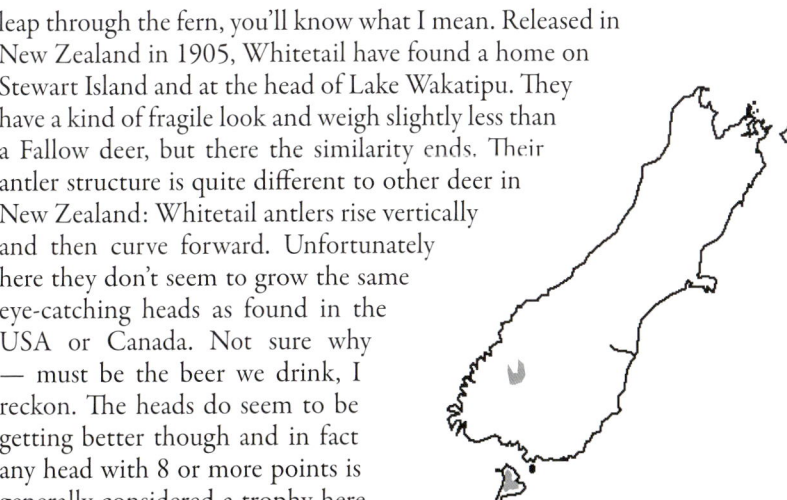

As well as having the most attractive skins of any of our deer species, they also deliver the nicest venison.

Obviously the does are so beautiful the stags feel they don't have to roar to attract them, although they are supposed to grunt – not that I have heard them. The rut usually begins about the start of May, which means that if you are a keen and wealthy hunter you can hunt Wapiti hybrids at the end of March, Reds at the beginning of April, then Sika and Fallow through April, before moving on to Whitetail, then having a break before the Rusa and Sambar kick into action in July and August!

On Stewart Island, Whitetails are often found around the coast and sometimes on the beaches, not for the sunbathing I can assure you, but evidently they eat the seaweed. They are challenging to bush stalk and a smart hunter will seek to find out where they are living and spend a significant time sitting watching. During the rut in particular the stags tend to move around a lot more.

Every New Zealand hunter should take a trip to Stewart Island to hunt Whitetail. Even if you don't come home with a magnificent trophy to impress your wife, you may collect a nice skin and you will probably see a kiwi or two and maybe even catch a fish. It's a great place.

SAMBAR

These are big mommas and they are tough. Built like miniature Sherman tanks and complete with armour some would say, a big stag could weigh as much as 250kg, generally larger than a Red stag. Thick set and heavy boned, their ability to absorb lead is legendary. They were introduced into New Zealand first in 1873, which makes them a bit late for a Treaty of Waitangi claim. There are only two places you can hunt Sambar: in the Rangiteiki district of the Manawatu and around the Mount Edgecumbe area in the Rotorua district. Note that Sambar in the Manawatu are

Three Sambar deer – they certainly look different to Reds.

managed by DoC and the Sambar foundation www.sambardeer.co.nz. There is a restricted season and hunting rights are balloted, unless you know a friendly farmer.

Sambar have a reputation for being hard to hunt, which is not surprising considering they prefer to feed at night, a fact that doesn't exactly help Nimrod the hunter. To add insult to injury they also have a great ability to hide in gorse, scrub and swamp, places you would agree are a little difficult to stalk through. In the not too distant past, most hunters got their thrills by dogging them, something that is frowned on today. Sambar definitely prefer not to be hunted with dogs, including the electric variety.

One hunting technique for Sambar is a carbon copy of that for Rusa – find a nice spot, take a pair of good binoculars and watch, but make sure you are there early, and try to spot them as they head back into the scrub at first light. Another productive method is to very slowly stalk feeding areas on dawn and dusk. While Sambar are supposed to breed throughout the year, July and August are generally regarded as being the best months to hunt them. A top trophy stag will have antlers at least 75cm (30 inches) long, have six points or more and will score over 200 on the Douglas score. They don't appear to give a roar of any description, but some very occasionally do make a 'belling' noise and the Sambar grunt is loud enough to give any hunter a start. There are a number of reasonable to good heads coming out each year now, but as it is difficult to get access to properties you may have your work cut out finding one. Whatever you do, use a rifle with plenty of grunt. And finally, after you have bust your gut getting a Sambar carcass out to eat the meat, you will probably regret your decision — from all accounts the dog will probably end up with it.

FIORDLAND DEER

A final thought about Fiordland. A trophy Wapiti/Red hybrid or Fiordland deer, as they are now called, is still a magnificent trophy and worthy of a place of honour on the wall. Besides, Fiordland is such a magical place that every Kiwi hunter owes it to himself to take at least one trip into its inspiring country. As William McHutcheson said many years ago, "The academic copestone of New Zealand's unapproachable curriculum is undoubtedly the mountains, lakes and valleys of Fiordland, and no New Zealander can henceforth call his education complete until he has taken the course."

(See www.fiordland.org.nz for information on Wapiti blocks.)

Be prepared — take some first aid.

Chapter 2 — GEAR

CLOTHING AND ACCESSORIES

Today you can head into the bush wearing clothes that Barry Crump could only dream of! With fabrics that are both windproof and in some cases also waterproof, the modern hunter has no excuse for heading into the bush with inadequate clothing. There are a number of manufacturers who produce excellent gear for the New Zealand hunter and my suggestion is that if you are serious regarding your hunting, you should invest in the best right from the start.

Firstly, some **DON'TS**

1] **Don't** wear jeans hunting — they are noisy and, once wet, stay wet and cold — a real trap for the young hunter. If you are wanting to make a fashion statement with jeans, just don't go hunting in them!

2] **Don't** under-dress. My policy is that it is always easier to take clothing off than to put it on. Alternatively, carry some extra clothing. Modern micro fleece tops take up so little room in your day bag that carrying one as extra insurance is no problem. Many a time I have left Taupo on a fine, clear morning only to be greeted by extreme cold and wet when hitting the hills. Local areas often have very localised weather patterns. One prime example would be the Waipunga Valley, east of Taupo. Generally if the weather is fine in Taupo it will be windy and raining there — you can count on it! If you haven't got it, you can't put it on.

3] **Don't** forget to take something waterproof to chuck in your bag in case the weather turns really sour as it so often does in the great New Zealand outdoors. If you are dry, life is much more pleasant.

4] **Don't** forget your space blanket. Hopefully you'll never need it, but it could save your life if you're caught out or have an accident. Space blankets, by the way, are a thin aluminium sheet that you can wrap around your body in an emergency to keep you warm and dry. Cost: approx. $6.00. I have inserted one in the butt of my rifles so I know I always have one with me.

5] **Don't** forget your map and compass. It's an interesting fact of life that people who are best prepared for any eventuality are probably the least likely to have things go wrong!

6] **Don't** forget to tell someone where you are going! Yes, we hunters don't like to think anyone may even suspect our hot spots, but it is prudent to let someone know of your intentions!

WHAT TO WEAR and TAKE

Some Suggestions:

Have a look at the gear available and ask around. Don't be in a hurry. Do buy quality gear and it will last you a long time. Over the years I have used and appreciated the products of New Zealand manufacturers such as Huntech, Stoney Creek and Swazi. Hunting and Fishing now have their own clothing line as well, as do the New Zealand Fishing and Shooting Pro Shops group. I'd encourage you to think seriously about what you buy, in terms of where it's made. Yes, you can purchase cheap options in clothing, but you may get what you pay for. More importantly, you may not be supporting New Zealand manufacturers who employ New Zealand workers. Buying cheap may be short-term gain for long-term pain. Economics aside, here's a list you might like to consider:

1] **Good quality leather boots,** although the lightweight cheaper versions are fine for bush hunting Sika etc. I have also used rubber Buller boots and similar; great for bush stalking, but not for walking long distances with a pack as they have no padding. There is a huge variety of boots around ... take your pick. Actually the best boots I ever had for bush stalking were lightweight leather ones from The Warehouse! I bought several pairs at the time and eventually they all wore out — unfortunately!

2] **Quality socks** such as Bridgedale. You spend a lot of time on your feet when hunting so make sure what you are walking on is good quality. Sore feet are no fun! Guaranteed to ruin a good hunt.

3] **Lightweight trousers or shorts,** the latter combined with polyester or polypropylene longs. Have had great feedback re Stoney Creek "Micro Tough" longs.

Well-dressed hunters, Tim Gale and Mike Fraser arrive back just on dusk. Note how the extra orange on Mike really stands out.

4] **Long or short-sleeved singlet** made of a polyester fabric, of which there are many on the market.

5] **Micro fleece tops, short or long sleeved, can be used as a singlet or taken as an extra** in case the weather turns cold, as often all you need initially is a singlet and a good quality top. These micro fleece tops are incredibly light and warm.

6] **Warm hat** — my preference is for an orange creation, made to stand out. However, I seldom wear a hat as I find they are too warm and seem to dull my senses. I prefer an orange sweat band around my head, which stops the rain drops running down my nose and adds a little extra orange. A hat is very useful in cold conditions — it also shows a lot more orange than a band. However, in my experience wearing a head band is not sufficient — you need significantly more orange to be seen.

7] **Polar fleece or windproof top** — some of these are also significantly waterproof. Polar fleece is a good choice as it's very quiet, although some of the later quality fabrics are also incredibly quiet, windproof and mainly waterproof. Seeing is believing. They also breathe which means you don't get wet from sweating.

8] **Waterproof jacket** — there are several ways to go here. For much of your hunting you can carry a lightweight waterproof jacket such as the "Extra Lite" garment Stoney Creek make, or you can wear a top that is windproof and mainly waterproof. However, if you head into places like Fiordland you will need something for extreme wet conditions such as seam-sealed garments made by Huntech, Swazi or Stoney Creek. The Swazi Tahr Anorak certainly has a great reputation, as do all their products. At times in Fiordland it's like walking under a waterfall for days on end, so you need something that keeps the wet out — obviously!

9] **Safety vest** — coloured orange, or a blaze orange garment i.e. jacket or shirt. If you're hunting in the public arena make sure you wear one, and don't cover it up when you put your rain jacket on. At least one hunter has lost his life because he made that mistake.

10] **Gaiters (or puttees)** — for over the tops of your boots to keep stones and twigs out. I prefer the neoprene variety as they are quiet and effective, but other designs are good. Some others designed for trampers can be very noisy, so make sure your gaiters are of a material that is quiet.

11] **Gloves** — I prefer fingerless gloves, especially for my right hand, except when I'm hunting Rusa and sitting for hours in freezing winter conditions. In those circumstances I'm the best-dressed Arctic hunter around! A good compromise may be a fingerless glove on the hand of your trigger finger and a full glove on the other hand or you could cut off the glove finger of your trigger finger!

12] **Quality day bag** — lots to choose from today. Mine is a Stoney Creek 2 in 1, but anything about 25–30 litres capacity is fine. I've tried a number of bags, but the reason I like the Stoney Creek product is that it has two compartments and is waterproof. Any smaller and you'll run out of space. I find now that I'm not meat hunting I tend to take a bit more gear, not that the extra weight is noticeable. Some guys like bum bags, so that's another option.

13] **Your Weapon** — Almost any modern centrefire rifle will do the job on deer, and plenty has been written about choice of weapons and calibres. When I am hunting just for meat I use a lighter calibre rifle like my Remington 600 in 22/250, but for trophy hunting I prefer my old custom built Remington 700 in 30/06. The key thing to remember is that shot placement and good bullets are <u>critical above all else</u>!

14] **Knife** — I personally prefer a smaller knife rather than a great big pig sticker or Bowie knife. In fact I reckon a knife with a drop point blade or semi-drop point blade about 9–12.5cm long is about right. With a knife that size I can gut deer, remove head skins and, if necessary, skin deer. Interestingly, when I was commercially hunting I used a Swiss Army pocket knife! Never needed anything else.

15] **Binoculars** — Over the years I've made do with lesser quality binoculars, but if I had my time again I'd buy the very best I could. It is absolutely amazing the difference that quality binoculars make in terms of what you can see. I'd say that right behind a good rifle and scope, a top quality pair of binoculars is the next most important piece of equipment you can buy. You may use your scope to fire at a few deer, but you will use your binoculars all the time, and more so today when there are few, if any, helicopters to keep the deer off the tops. What power? Well I'd buy either 8 or 10 power. Anything above 10 power and you will find it difficult to hold steady unless your binoculars are the image stabilising variety. The latter are great, but may be a bit too bulky for some. The advantage is you can use a higher power yet retain a still image.

16] **Bipod** — I have always been a bit sceptical about these, as most of my hunting has been in the bush, but now with few choppers around to scare animals away these are a useful piece of equipment to take, especially if you are shooting at any distance. They weigh very little and my clients find them of great assistance.

17] **Range finder** — I'm astounded at how useful a range finder is. While I have done most of my hunting in the bush, I thought I was pretty good at estimating distances at long range. Not so! Using a range finder showed me just how far out some of my guesstimates were — just as well I didn't fire at the deer without knowing the distance. I could have missed by a country mile! A very useful addition to the gear then is a quality range finder.

While I have reservations about extreme long range shooting as practised by Greg Duley and disciples, I believe they can teach us a thing or two about shooting accurately at longer ranges. For them a range finder is a critical piece of equipment and I can see a huge advantage in knowing exactly how far away game is, coupled with a rifle that is accurate and effective at these ranges and fired by a hunter who is a competent shot! All credit to them for breaking new ground in New Zealand, even if I prefer the close quarter encounters in the bush where hormone-driven, love-crazed Sika stags are breathing down my throat at twenty metres or less.

Now that the helicopters are no longer blitzing the deer on the tops, hunters are finding more animals out in the open and consequently at longer ranges. Again however, can I stress the importance here of buying quality gear — you may pay more initially, but believe me you won't regret it down the track. Buy good gear and it will last you a lifetime. Buy poorer quality and you will be forever comparing it with someone else's superior gear! And they will be seeing and getting the animals, not you.

18] **GPS (Global Positioning System)** – There are a number of excellent GPSs available now with the ability to tell a hunter where he is to within a few metres. My personal view is that you should buy one with an electronic compass if at all possible, because you need to know where north is to orient the GPS correctly. While a normal GPS will not do this until you have moved a bit, it may be quite difficult in some terrain where you cannot move too far without losing contact with your satellites. I normally use a compass to orient my GPS to the north, as mine doesn't come complete with an electronic compass.

A GPS will give you more confidence as you head into the bush to go into new areas. It will enable you to stay out longer and help you to mark key areas such as clearings. They are not idiot-proof though, and are of little use to those who would quickly get lost in my backyard! They are definitely not a substitute for common sense. They're a wonderful new piece of equipment though, so why not take advantage of new technology? And don't forget spare batteries, your map and a compass – they may come in handy some time!

19] **Mountain Radio** – On some longer trips it may be advisable to take a mountain radio, not only for weather forecasts, but for emergencies. These radios are cheap to hire and weigh very little (equal in size and weight to a pack of butter) and in fact I have carried them with me on a solo trip. You simply follow instructions to set up the aerial and they have a sked every night at a predetermined time. The operators will relay messages. When you are camped kilometres from civilisation it is great to hear a friendly voice telling you the latest rugby score or the good news of an anti cyclone arriving the next day. They are also planning to make available the option of a personal locator beacon for a small charge, which is a great idea. Check out their web site for details of a mountain radio contact near you. www.nzlsar.org.nz/mrs/wmrs/nzmrs.htm

Tim checking out his Garmin Etrex GPS. These are an invaluable aid to today's hunter. If used correctly they show you where you are, and will tell you what direction camp is, plus other useful information.

In My Day Bag

When I was meat hunting, I travelled light — rifle, ammo, carry belt and knife. Now on a day trip I carry a bit more gear:

1] GPS (and spare batteries), compass and map.

2] Knife (sharp) and sharpener.

3] Camera.

4] Mini tripod for camera that can be attached to branches etc so I can take pictures of myself in a scenic setting or with an animal. You'll be surprised how much you use it.

5] Space blanket and other emergency gear such as waterproof matches and a short piece of candle.

6] Rope — a couple of metres.

Author's son, Andrew, with the author's day bag and basic equipment carried for a hunt. From left: Lightweight rain coat, snack food, bags for venison, scope cover, polypropylene balaclava, mini tripod, head light and spare batteries, camera, space blanket, matches, rope, carry belt, knife sharpener, GPS and compass, first aid kit, lighter and spare ammo in the belt bag. A map also is essential if you are not familiar with an area.

7] Small first aid kit.

8] Carry belt.

9] Lightweight raincoat.

10] Warm orange hat — great for when the weather turns sour. If it is summer time, I sometimes take instead a wide brim hat as protection from the sun, especially if I am sitting in the open for long periods of time.

11] Torch and spare batteries — I prefer the headlamp variety as it means my hands are completely free. There are a number of different designs available. If you hunt on the tops a lot you may want a light that throws a beam some distance. For those who hunt in the bush this is not so critical.

12] An old pillowslip or plastic bags in which to put your meat.

13] Food.

It's cool to be orange — the hinds will love you.

Chapter 3   PERSONAL PREPARATION

You are on the hunt of the year and you have just spotted a big stag. He's sneaked out into a small gap in the bush and he's restless, or he's just emerged onto a clearing on a far ridge. You may have a window of opportunity of only a few seconds in the bush and a little more out in the open. What will you do?

If you call in a big Sika stag, for example, he may barrel in or sneak in. You'll have very quick look at him, first to make certain it is a stag, before you decide whether to shoot him and where. In these few seconds he too is appraising the situation and may vanish just as quickly as he came. If you are not familiar with your rifle and have not practised your shooting, chances

Simon Heard checking the rifle before heading off for a hunt. Note the suppressor built by McColl Arms & Engineering www.mae.co.nz. They certainly make a huge difference to noise and recoil.

Fallow deer venison is almost on a par with Whitetail. Note different colours of the deer.

A large Fallow stag like this big boy, shot by Chen Zhi Hui, has a beautiful skin that would look great in a den or on your floor.

Tim with a magnificent Sika head shot Easter 2006 DS 188 2/8. The smile says it all.

Tim dressed for April hunting – note use of high visibility clothing. It pays to be prepared when venturing into the hills. Day pack contains wet weather gear and food. The rifle is also equipped with a Harris bipod.

are you'll muff the opportunity. He'll be gone before you remember to put the bolt down or put the safety off. If you don't believe me take an unfamiliar rifle out for a day and see how easy it is to remember where everything is – like driving someone else's car!

Similarly, you may spot a big stag as he drifts onto a clearing at, say, an honest 340 metres. You have a quick look at him in the binoculars before deciding you want his head on your wall. You have maybe twenty seconds or less as he is a bit restless and is heading for deeper cover. You check your range finder, but realise your rifle is sighted in for 150 metres and you don't know how low the bullet will drop by the time it has reached the stag. You also haven't practised your long range shooting or even practised while sitting down. Tough – you fire in a bit of a panic and you know immediately in your heart you have missed. Sad really, and unnecessary too, because with a little forethought and preparation the outcome could have been so different.

My philosophy is to do as much as I can even before I go out hunting to eliminate any possible factors that may make a difference as to whether I get an animal or not. For example, I know where my rifle is shooting and I practise my shooting. I have taped to the outside of the rear lens of my scope the bullet drop figures for up to 500 metres, so I know instantly if that once in a lifetime trophy is 428 metres away, just how much I need to hold over him to connect. I also wear soft clothing and try not to have anything that rattles in my pockets or day bag.

Anyway here are three basic tips that will go a long way to help ensure that you will bag that big one the next time you run across him.

A good outcome for a hunt starts even <u>before</u> you hit the field.

Know where your rifle is shooting

This gives you great confidence! I'd suspect a number of guys go into the hills without having sighted in their rifle, and consequently they miss or mess up a shot and wound an animal. An investment of a couple of hours in making sure your rifle is properly sighted in is well worth it. It gives you great confidence to know that if you have to fire at an animal at 300 metres or so, for example, you will be able to connect.

For the record, I generally sight my rifles in to hit the button at 240 metres (approx 260 yards). This means my 30/06, shooting a 165gr projectile at about 2930fps, is about 4cm high at 50 metres, 7.5cm high at 100 metres, on the button at 240m and only 10cm low at 275m and 25cm low at 320m. With my .22/250 and the 53 gr Barnes bullet, I am 2cm high at 50 metres, 6.5cm high at 100 metres, 6cm high at 235 metres (250 yards), on the button at 300 yards and 23cm low at 400 yards. If I have had any success at hunting, I'd say one key reason is that I have been meticulous about knowing where my rifle is shooting. This was true even in my meat hunting days when the number of animals was higher than today, but a missed shot could be pretty costly. I used to spend hours at the range working up loads and tuning my rifles so they shot accurately and consistently, even though I was mainly bush hunting.

I know that for most bush stalking your shots are generally at less than an honest 40 metres and so some prefer to sight their rifles in for say 100 metres. That's OK if you can guarantee all your shots will be at close range, but what if you see a big stag at 275 metres? Your rifle will be shooting about 30 centimetres low. Best to sight in for a longer distance and take advantage of the trajectory of your rifle.

While on the subject of sighting in, my practice is to begin at 25 metres by bore sighting first. With the rifle held securely, remove the bolt and then align the bore with a distinctive object at about 100 metres distance. Then, without disturbing the rifle, look through the sights. If they are not aligned correctly make the correct adjustments until the crosshairs line up with the alignment of the bore. Because this will only be approximate, you next need to fire a shot at 25 metres, then adjust your sights so your point of impact is spot on at that distance. Then move back to 100 metres and fire some more shots, one at a time, until you are approximately 7.5cm high or whatever height you want your bullets to strike. I strongly recommend sighting in finally at the 100 metres distance as every error at 25m is multiplied four times or more at 100 metres.

A great web site to check out in this respect is huntingnut.com You can download for free their "Point Blank" programme that will give you information about different bullets, powders, primers and you can enter in your own data for individual loads and print out the trajectories of your loads for different ranges etc. That way you will know exactly where the bullet will hit at 300, 400 and 500 metres etc, plus velocities, energies, bullet travel time etc. at these ranges so you will have no excuses! An excellent web

A Whitetail doe in the bush. You may have only one chance to get your deer. This is what all that preparation was for.

site for targets is www.mytargetz.com.

Practise good trigger control

This is CRITICAL!! If you pull your shots by jerking the trigger, you will most likely hit air or trees and possibly wound a deer. This usually happens when you line up a big stag. However, practise dry firing and you'll find your shooting improves significantly. Dry firing means firing on an EMPTY shell in your chamber. The object is to train yourself to squeeze the trigger in such a way that you don't jerk it, but release it gently and consistently. You can do this at home in your lounge and you can use the same shell a number of times. Imagine you are out hunting and you see a deer. Your imaginary deer could be the neighbour's cat or a rock. Close your bolt, raise your rifle and "fire" as you would in the field. When you begin you will notice how inconsistent your shooting is, but by practising your dry firing you will learn to do the right things consistently. Because you will have better trigger control, you are more likely to hit your animal where you want to and not end up with a shot in its guts or back end, or worse, have it disappear into the scrub unscathed. A note of caution here: when doing your dry firing practice DON'T do it in view of the public — be discreet!

Practise your shooting

Good shots become better shots by practising. Go to the range and spend a few dollars shooting a .22. Make up cardboard rabbits or deer and imagine you are in live shooting conditions. Believe me, it's often not the animals at 100 metres you miss; it's the ones at 20 metres. You spend hundreds of dollars on a trip — spend a few as an investment by honing your shooting skills. I believe one key aspect of being a successful hunter is to eliminate all the possible things that can go wrong, that may prevent you getting an animal. There are many things you have no control over, such as which tree the stag inconveniently stands behind, or which way the wind swirls, but work on eliminating the things that can go wrong and are under your control and your chances of success will improve. Sharpening up your shooting skills is one of these. A better idea is to get out after rabbits or try some varmint shooting. Even taking out the .22 for a walk and shooting rabbits or hares will improve your shooting no end. Practice makes perfect.

Have fun — but not at someone else's expense.

Chapter 4

FIVE TIPS FROM A GUNSMITH TO IMPROVE THE ACCURACY OF YOUR RIFLE

Grateful thanks to Dean Maisey for this article. Dean, who hails from Tauranga, is a keen hunter and has a reputation of being one of the best gunsmiths around. See addendum for a list of gunsmiths.

OVERVIEW

Accuracy in modern hunting rifles can pretty much be considered a result of the combination of good barrels and bedding, proper scope alignment, good triggers and quality ammunition, provided of course that the shooter

There is a huge range of good firearms available today. Here Ken Coombes, manager of Hunting & Fishing, Taupo, explains the benefits of a quality rifle like this Sako to a customer. However, note that most factory produced rifles can benefit hugely from a tune up by a good gunsmith.

is reasonably competent and can do his/her part. For the sake of this article we are basically dealing with deer-hunting rifles, so the term "accurate" will be deemed to mean a rifle/ammo combination capable of producing 3 or 5 shot groups of 1" or less at 100 yards.

With the improvement of manufacturing methods in recent years as well as a plethora of rifle reviews and advertising in hunting and shooting magazines, many hunters think you can just go out and buy a new factory rifle with some factory loaded ammunition and start shooting one-hole groups all day long. Sadly, in the real world this is not quite the case. A lot of hunters may only be able to afford a second-hand rifle, or may have one handed down to them from a friend or family member as a favour or gift. With "used" rifles the potential for wear and neglect related problems is huge. While there are entire books written on the subject of rifle accuracy I have only enough space here to go over some of the major points. Suffice to say though that when you are working on rifles as your full-time job, you do come to realise there are a lot of imperfections or "things left to be desired" in the common factory "sporters" or ex-military rifles. It's a general rule-of-thumb that you get what you pay for, and with rifles this is often the case. However, by spending your money wisely with a good gunsmith or gun-dealer, you may be able to achieve your goals without breaking the budget.

Barrel

Just as a good motor is the heart of any performance car, the barrel is the heart of any good rifle. Basically, if the barrel is suspect then all the other "bells and whistles" type alterations will amount to zero (or insufficient) improvement. If it's an old rifle where the barrel has fired several thousand rounds and is so badly worn that it is considered "shot-out", or the barrel has been neglected by shooting corrosive ammunition and/or lack of cleaning, resulting in a rusty or pitted bore, then the remedy is a new barrel (or a new rifle). A barrel with a rough bore is never going to shoot very well. What is required is a nice cleanly rifled bore, with a smooth surface finish, which is (preferably) perfectly straight. A lot of factory grade barrels <u>are not</u> perfectly straight, but can often be made to shoot acceptably well despite this.

Other common barrel problems are: poorly reamed chambers with the throat area not concentric (or in line with) the bore, poorly "crowned" barrels, and the occasional "oil bulge" in a bore near the muzzle (usually from firing a shot through a bore without first patching out the protective oil layer that had been applied previously).

The latter two problems can usually be remedied by the suitably equipped gunsmith by shortening the barrel slightly and recrowning it properly. As for the former, sorry but the solution is a new barrel.

All barrels, regardless of contour/profile, vibrate when they are fired. Obviously the thin, "soda straw" type barrels will vibrate and oscillate more at the muzzle than the big heavy "truck axle" type ones seen on target and benchrest rifles. If the barrel is free-floated clear of the forend then the fitting of an "over the barrel" type suppressor can help to stiffen the barrel and reduce some of the magnitude of these vibrations. The fitting to the barrel of a "muzzle-brake" or a "barrel tuner" device can also make the barrel shoot with more consistent accuracy than it did before. A good gunsmith who understands rifle accuracy should be able to undertake this sort of work for you. "General engineers", in 95% of cases, do not have the special-purpose tools and jigs required to complete custom barrel work to an acceptable standard, and efficiently. Use a professional gunsmith who is fully set-up for this type of work. Do it right the first time and save yourself some money and hassles.

Of course there are drawbacks to consider with either of these options. All will add to the overall length of the rifle, suppressors add weight as well (but reduce noise and recoil), and muzzle brakes also add noise (but reduce recoil). Consult your gunsmith on the best option for you.

If you have to fit a new barrel then it makes sense to use only very good quality barrels. As the time taken to custom-fit them is still the same, it seems foolish to try to save $20–$30 on a "cheapy" barrel and risk all the time and effort going to waste.

There are some good custom barrel makers out there, some real shockers too. I personally have had a good run from True Flite, Shilen, Douglas, etc..

Bedding

A rifle's action, properly fitted and bedded into the stock, should be completely free of any bending or torsional stresses when the action screws are done up tight. If the bedding of your rifle has not been properly executed, then the action can be warped or distorted when the rifle's action screws are tightened. This can cause the rifle's bolt to not sit correctly into place, causing poor bolt lug and sear contact/alignment, and in some cases poor bedding can cause a stock to crack behind and under the action from recoil forces. "Barrel vibrations" can also be affected if there is some degree of twisting or "bowing" of the action.

In most cases for hunting rifles, the barrels often shoot to a more consistent point of impact with a free-floated barrel. Usually this is best accomplished by epoxy "bedding" the rifle's action to the stock, allowing the compound to set with the barrel sitting correctly at the "half-depth line" in the forend. Later, when the metalwork is removed from the stock after the epoxy has

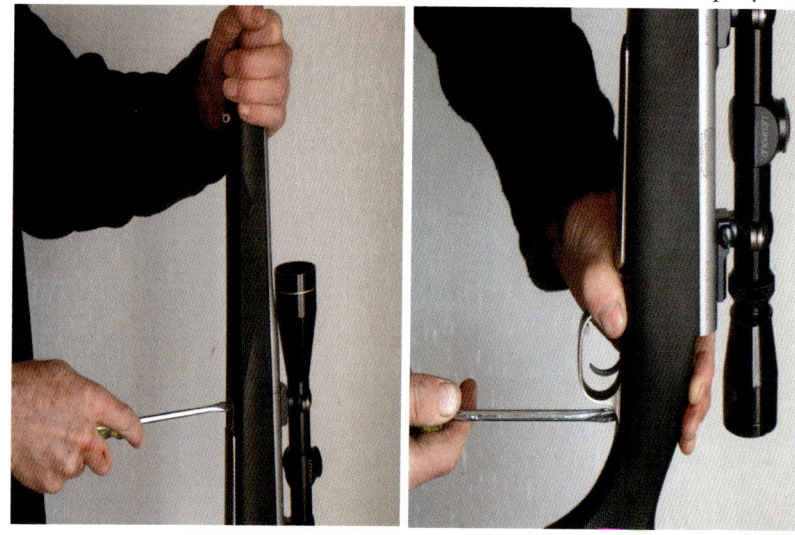

Left: A good test: First tighten the tang (rear) screw and hold the rifle with your finger around the barrel as indicated. Then alternately tighten and loosen the screw that goes into the front of the action. As you do, if you feel the barrel moving or flexing at all, then the bedding of your rifle may need some attention and accuracy may be affected. If the action or barrel are flexed by pressure be sure accuracy will suffer.Right: Here, tighten up the screw that goes into the front of the action. Then tighten up the tang (rear) screw and loosen it, while holding your finger on the rear of the action. If the rear of the action flexes or moves significantly, again you have a problem – your action may be bending when the screws are tightened and this will affect accuracy.

set, the barrel channel can be scraped or sanded out to an even clearance of about 0.040" (1.0mm) or more. There are some exceptions where the occasional barrel may shoot better with a "pressure point" bedding system (explained later in this section). This can sometimes help if the barrel has possibly been mechanically straightened at some stage and/or will not shoot well free-floated.

When wooden stocks are "glass bedded" the bedding job can later be ruined if the action screws are over-tightened, causing the wooden fibres under the compound to compress, which then allows the action to distort again. To prevent this a process called "pillar bedding" is often used. This involves incorporating custom-machined aluminium sleeves (or "pillars") over the action screws, which maintain a set distance between the underside of the rifle's action and the top surface of the "bottom metal" (trigger guard, floorplate, etc.). To do the job correctly the pillars and the action must be bedded into the stock at the same time in one operation. Trying to do the job in two stages usually results in a substandard fit and finish, as different epoxy "mixes" will always set and contract slightly at a different rate to the original/previous application. Also, the magazine box should have a slight clearance at either the top or lower edges and be clear to move freely on all sides so that it does not bear tightly or contact with the stock in such a way that it acts as a "recoil lug", which may then cause the stock to crack in the "web area".

A lot of factory rifles, "slapped together", incorporate a "pressure point" bedding system, whereby the barrel is supported midway along its length (usually near the forend tip), by a raised bedding pad/s inside the barrel channel of the stock. This applies a slight upward pressure to the barrel, which in turn dampens out some of the "whip" or "barrel vibrations" when the rifle is fired. While this can sometimes help the rifle shoot better three shot groups, successive firing often causes the shots to start "walking up" the target as the barrel heats up and expands lengthways, increasing the upward pressure from the bedding pad. The other disadvantages of this system are that the rifle must be sighted in again after the rifle has been completely dismantled for cleaning or service, as the point of impact can be altered if the action screws are not tightened back up to exactly the same position every time. Likewise the warping of the forend wood or compression in the bedding area of wooden stocks can also cause the pressure point force to vary, thereby shifting the point of impact over time, often without the shooter being aware of it. For this reason most shooters prefer to have the rifle's barrel free-floating.

Experimentation must then be undertaken to see which factory-manufactured or custom-loaded ammunition shoots the most accurate groups in the rifle with the barrel free-floated.

I would like to state, for the record, that I feel that glass/epoxy bedding should be left to a qualified or competent rifle/gunsmith. If you are not confident you can do the job yourself to a high standard don't do it!! Amateur attempts at bedding often result in a poorly executed and finished job, especially if the guy doing the job has a shortage of suitable craft-tools and accessories. In some cases the action has been "permanently glued" into the stock, much to the embarrassment of the "tyro". Sometimes the only remedy can be to cut the stock to separate it from the action. Hardly ideal!

As mentioned previously though, a "bedding job" can be a waste of time and money if the barrel is stuffed, so have this checked out first.

Scope Alignment

Like a rifle's action, the scope should be mounted securely, but in a way that the body/tube is free from any bending or stresses. To achieve this, the scope rings must be in perfect alignment in all axes. This can often mean "shimming" the scope bases to get the heights of the base tops the same, and/or reaming the internal 1" diameter hole in the scope rings with a special-purpose 1" diameter "scope ring alignment reamer". Alternatively, the scope can be mounted in rings that incorporate a self-aligning plastic insert, of the design by Burris or Sako. These rings, properly installed, align the inserts directly off the scope tube body and are then tightened into place, providing an easily achieved stress-free set-up. Ideally the reticle (or "cross-hairs") of the scope should be square with the central axis and "flats" of the action.

An incorrectly installed scope with a "stressed" body can cause point of impact changes with variations in temperature, and may affect the internal mechanisms or the integrity of the scope. Considering that most scope tubes now are made from lightweight aluminium, it is quite possible to permanently damage or bend the scope tube body due to poor scope mounting or installation procedure.

With scopes on high-powered rifles you should ideally buy the best you can afford. Cheap scopes with dodgy adjustment and reticle return-spring mechanisms will end up giving you hassles and can sometimes be the source of unexplained "flyers" or accuracy problems. Once again you generally get what you pay for. The better quality lenses and coatings on the more expensive models will usually help you to see the target/animal more clearly in low or failing light conditions, whereas the cheap models will often let you down. What looks okay in the gunshop, often is not so okay in the low light of the bush or a late evening hunt. Buy quality and cry about it once.

Trigger

A lot of factory-produced rifles now are issued with triggers that release with a pull weight of anywhere from 3½–7lbs, and with a "safe" amount of sear engagement. This is largely to counter the US liability laws that we are all too aware of. I generally consider a trigger pull weight of 2¾lbs to be ideal and safe for a deerstalking rifle, and a good compromise pull weight. Generally I would alter a standard "two-lever" style trigger to release at a lighter pull weight, down to about 2lbs or so, only if I knew the rifle's owner and was assured he/she was doing mainly long range shooting and could keep the rifle's mechanism in a clean and well-maintained condition. If a guy wants a significantly lighter trigger, then a "three-lever" style target trigger may be required.

Once again, can I strongly recommend that trigger alterations be performed only by a suitably equipped, qualified or competent rifle/gunsmith. Each gunsmith has his own liability to consider in this area, and it's at his own discretion what he considers an acceptable setting for a particular trigger mechanism.

Of course it must be stated clearly that a smooth, light-releasing trigger, will not technically make a rifle more "accurate", but it does allow the shooter to control the rifle more easily to release the shot without "straining" or "flinching".

Ammunition

The quality and consistency of the rifle ammunition being used has a major influence on the accuracy of the rifle. The quality of the ammunition components, bullet alignment, and minimising shot-to-shot velocity variations, all affect accuracy potential. Also, as each individual rifle barrel vibrates slightly differently to another, even when fired with the same ammunition, so the results may be very poor or very good with different rifles. The rule-of-thumb therefore is to find a particular factory load with the bullet weight you desire that shoots the best in your rifle, once the previous four mentioned sections (barrel/bedding/scope/trigger) have been attended to. This may mean trying half a dozen or more types of factory-loaded ammunition in your rifle's calibre of different makes and even different bullet weights. If your results are still not satisfactory, or if you choose, then custom-loaded ammunition to specifically suit your rifle is the final solution. This can be done yourself if you have the necessary equipment and skills to complete the task of loading and testing safely. Otherwise ammunition reloaders such as "Custom Cartridges" in Taupo can be hired to do the job for you. Contact them for their rates for this service on 07 3784593 or go to www.customcartridges.co.nz

CONCLUSION

In closing I must state clearly that this was not intended to be "How to build a super-accurate benchrest rifle", or something similar. It would take a whole book to do the subject justice. However, I have included a lot of the basic information that most shooters should understand about their rifles and how they work, or more importantly, how a gunsmith can improve their performance. Searching for the source/s of accuracy problems is really just a process of elimination, but going through the process in the correct order will determine whether you end up wasting money or not.

Finally, keep your rifle in as clean and tidy condition as possible at all times. Lightly oiled, not "drowned" in the stuff. Clean the bore on a regular basis with a good "copper solvent" to remove the copper jacket fouling material. This will aid accuracy and prolong the life of the barrel also. Patch the bore out free of oil before you fire a shot. Oil when not in use.

Clean your "stainless" rifles just as you would a "blued" rifle. "Stainless" in rifle steel does not mean "maintenance-free" – you just have a little more margin for laziness about cleaning than with the blued rifles. Look after your rifle and your gear, and it will look after you when you need to make the shot that counts in the field. (Dean Maisey's website is www.gunsmith.co.nz.)

Chapter 5   TIPS ON KNIVES

Knives are as personal as rifles. Some guys like them flashy, others functional, and yet others think the bigger the better! In purchasing a knife for hunting you first need to ask what you going to use it for. If it's just for gutting deer and removing the head skin if you are fortunate to shoot a trophy, you won't need a super long blade. In fact my observation would be that most young hunters purchase knives that are far too big, believing I suppose that "the knife maketh the hunter," or, at the very least, a big knife hung on the belt will, in some mystical way, bring them success. Large knives may look impressive to some, but deer are unlikely to be impressed. As stated before, I prefer a drop point blade of about 9–12.5cm long, as this style blade generally won't dig into a deer's stomach as you gut it. A smaller knife also makes it easier to head-skin trophies. I've never used a knife with a gut hook, but many swear by them and say they make gutting animals a lot easier.

A selection of knives available to hunters, compliments of Hunting & Fishing Taupo. From bottom left, Wheeler, Gerber and Winchester fixed blade drop point, Svord utility, drop point and boning knives, Buck drop point with gut hook, Leatherman, Gerber and Buck lock blade pocket knives and a Buck utility knife.

One important issue is the ability of a knife to hold its edge. Many years ago, when I was meat hunting one day down Lake Hauroko in Fiordland, my mate Ronald told me he'd buy me a fancy German knife of a well known brand if I shot a stag in a particular bit of bush we called the "Sure Thing". I'd seen these knives advertised in hunting magazines and had drooled over them many a time with him, but never thought I'd be in a position to get one. However, this was my lucky day and success came my way only a few minutes after I'd left the boat. In due course Ronald bought me my very, very expensive knife. I was rapt. It had a fantastic design, beautiful antler handle, fancy scabbard and I thought all my Christmases had come at once. But oh, it had one major problem: it wouldn't hold its edge. I'd gut half a deer and it would be blunt! With stags in the roar it was even worse as I tried to cut their thick hides. After numerous attempts to discover a remedy, I gave up in disgust and sent it back to Germany with a fairly terse note. It was returned, sharpened by the factory, with a note saying I was sharpening it the wrong way. Guess what — it made no difference. Was I hosed off! It was then back to the old faithful Swiss army knife. While Swiss army knives are great, I now prefer a knife with a fixed blade: they are a bit safer.

I've learned over the years to buy quality gear, because you will never regret it. I'd encourage anyone to spend a bit of extra money and buy a good knife. Sure you can buy cheaper ones, but somewhere along the track you'll say to yourself, "Why didn't I buy a decent knife?"

One New Zealand knife maker I have lot of respect for is Bryan Baker of Svord. I used to think that with a name like Svord, the knives must have come from overseas! Not so: Bryan is a New Zealander who has been making knives here since 1982. He makes a large variety of knives from a 3 inch Peasant knife, to an 11 inch Von Tempsky Bowie, as well as the standard drop point, skinning and cutlery knives etc. That Von Tempsky "machine" looks very impressive and imposing, believe you me! You probably won't need it for hunting — well not for deer anyway! Bryan's knives are all custom crafted from quality Swedish cutlery steel and have gained a great reputation for being easy to sharpen and for keeping their edge. Take his Peasant knife, for example — his blades pass the 90 degree flex test with no edge cracking and they will also cut a ¼ inch soft steel bolt with no edge damage! My good hunting friend, John Clarke, is a butcher by trade and reckons the Svord knives are the best he has ever used, and the "American Fighting Knives" publication rated their durability and edge-holding as "outstanding".

For most of us, getting a good edge can be a frustrating experience. Bryan has given some vital tips on how to sharpen a knife.

The Craftsman's Method Of Sharpening (Svord) Knives

Precision sharpening is a delicate operation: easy after practice, but to obtain first-class results with your knife the following procedure should be observed.

Referring to the diagram, select the grade of "Indian" or "Arkansas" stone according to the degree of coarseness of the "sawtooth" pattern desired. Take the knife in your usual working hand, lay it at an angle of 10–20 degrees to the stone, using the fingers of your free hand to apply mild pressure to the blade.

Draw the knife across the stone as if slicing it from the haft to the point. Turn the knife over and treat the other side in the same manner. Between ten to fifteen strokes to both sides should produce a very sharp durable edge, provided the correct angle and even finger pressure on the blade is maintained throughout the operation. Test for sharpness by slicing a newspaper sheet — the cut should be easy and no catching or ripping should occur. Look at the edge of the blade under a bright light. Dull edges will be visible and shiny. If the test fails, it's back to the stone.

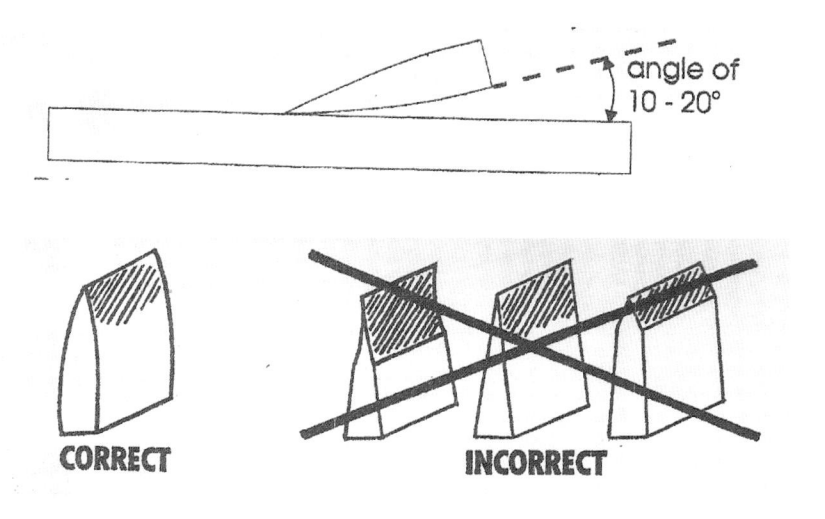

Caring For Your Knife: Some Vital Svord Tips

1] Never wash your knife in a dishwasher.

2] Never leave your knife wet or in water at any time or the knife will tarnish.

3] Always cut on a chopping board and not directly on the stainless steel bench top.

4] To wash your knife, run it under boiling water, as this imparts a bluish tinge to the steel.

5] To sharpen your knife we recommend abrasive sharpeners such as diamond steel or stone, traditional oil stone, India stone or Arkansas stone. Never use a Butcher's steel as it is designed to align the edge on soft steel knives.

6] If appropriate, store your knife in knife block or in a drawer separate from other cutlery to avoid it being damaged.

7] Some knives have rare exotic woods as handles. Occasionally you should polish them with furniture oil or boiled linseed oil.

8] If your knife tarnishes, use a green Scotch Brite pad to clean it.

The Svord web site is www.svord.com

The author with an 8 point Sika that missed the record book by ½ point! In this case he brought out the head, headskin, back steaks and hindquarters.

A magnificent 8 point Sika stag – you don't see too many like this, and they generally don't stop to check out the scenery! (Photo: B Ramsay)

Fly and Gun

Hunting & Fishing
NEW ZEALAND™

Taupo's Specialist Outdoors Store

See us for a complete range of...

- FRESHWATER TACKLE
- SALTWATER TACKLE
- FIRE ARMS AND AMMUNITION
- ALL YOUR CAMPING NEEDS
- OUTDOOR AND CASUAL CLOTHING
- FISHING LICENCES
- HUNTING PERMITS
- PROFESSIONAL FLY FISHING GUIDE SERVICES
- BOAT CHARTERS
- HUNTING GUIDES

FLY AND GUN

27 Gascoigne Street, **Taupo**
Phone: **07 378 4449** Fax: 07 378 4479
www.huntingandfishing.co.nz

Chapter 6

TO HUNT AND RETURN — DEVELOPING SAFE HUNTING PRACTICE

Suggested behaviour for minimising the likelihood of a hunting accident — used by permission of New Zealand Police.

See www.police.govt.nz/service/firearms/safehunting for the full booklet or ask your local firearms officer. This is a very worthwhile publication.

"While as a basic premise the shooter is always responsible for the shooting, and it is incumbent on the shooter to fully identify their target and comply with the New Zealand Arms Code, it is possible to identify, from the analysis of the deaths of deer hunters, specific behaviours that might be described as "protective". They are listed below in descending order of frequency in which the corresponding contributing factor appears (that is, the first is the most common contributing factor).

1] A hunter must not shoot at shape, sound or colour, including those belonging to a deer, without confirming that their target is a deer.

2] A wise hunter will wear clothing that contrasts with the environment, including deer in that environment.

3] When hunting together with a companion, cease hunting if visual contact with that companion is lost, and do not resume hunting until visual contact is made and confirmed.

4] Hunters must develop a self awareness that enables them to identify buck/stag fever in themselves, and counteract it with extra care when hunting.

5] Use binocular vision to identify the target; use the scope only to place the shot.

6] Snap shooting (as defined in this paper) is to be avoided unless target identification is complete.

7] If an area is obviously heavily occupied by other hunters, consider going hunting elsewhere.

8] Hunters should undergo hunter-specific training.

9] Hunters should belong to a club. Club membership is most likely to be the source of training and peer guidance.

10] Hunters should agree on hunting areas ("blocks"), with a clearly defined "no fire zone" between areas. Do not hunt outside the agreed area, including on the way back to camp.

11] If a linear boundary is agreed (for example a ridge line or creek), no shots may be fired toward or over that boundary line.

12] If it is absolutely necessary for one hunter to knowingly move into another's area, perhaps because of an emergency, do not stalk into the area. The hunter should enter in such a way that it is obvious they are not a deer.

13] Do not move into the firing zone or arc of fire of a hunting companion.

14] Sight more than a single part of the deer and confirm it as the target.

15] Minimise the likelihood of colour similar to that of a deer being visible.

16] Do not shoot when others are known to be in the firing zone.

17] When hunting together with a companion in parallel, keep sight of each other, maintain an arc of fire 180 degrees away form your hunting companion with a "no fire zone" between shooters, including forward and back.

18] When hunting together with a companion, and taking turns hunting, the non-hunting companion does not resume hunting until mutually agreed.

19] Hunting is not a time to fool around. Do not behave like a deer knowing your mate is hunting nearby. He may end up hunting you.

20] If carrying a deer carcass, cover it in some way so that it is clearly contrasted with the environment, including deer in that environment.

Safety Tips when around Vehicles and Huts (The Author)

Vehicles: Always carry your firearm with the bolt open or separate when transporting it in a vehicle. If you are ever stopped by the police and your rifle has the bolt down as if ready to fire, they will have justifiable cause for concern.

Also when transporting your rifle in a helicopter always remove the bolt. At the very least it gives the pilot a good impression. Make sure you do have it in your gear though!

Around huts and camps: Always leave your rifle with either the bolt open or out, even if it is lying on a bed or standing up against a wall. Here's a good rule we always observe – NEVER pick up someone else's firearm unless you first ask permission, even if that person is your best mate. And then treat it as if it were loaded and check it when you pick it up.

Treat all firearms as loaded.

Chapter 7 FROM THE HUNTING DOCTOR

Special thanks to Dr Tim Coulter, from Taupo, who contributed the following medical information. Tim is a personal friend and a keen hunter, whose comments come from a vast personal experience and knowledge. Grateful thanks also to the New Zealand Mountain Safety Council for the use of the illustrations here. See **www.mountainsafety.org.nz** for their informative website.

INTRODUCTION

Most hunters who regularly go into the bush do so for many years without injury and gradually become complacent. Sooner or later an incident is likely to arise where help will be needed. The topic has become personal for me as I am currently nursing a knee injury from a six metre fall while hunting alone this last roar. The following is a brief overview of the major injuries a hunter is likely to face, the initial treatment and when to call for help.

Those of us who take up hunting face a unique set of dangers. Most hunt on their own and try to find the most inaccessible areas where others would not go. We carry powerful weapons capable of inflicting terrible injury and we sometimes move about in the bush over rough ground in poor light. Injuries are therefore not infrequent and the constraints of isolation, weather and terrain mean that help is not easily available. Being stuck in cold wet bush with an injury such as a broken leg, for days at a time, is an unpleasant and memorable experience, if you are lucky enough to survive. Having a cell phone, mountain radio, locator beacon or someone at home who knows where you are and when to expect you back can be the difference between life and death.

If you are hunting in a group your chances of surviving an injury are greatly enhanced if you or your mates have some first aid knowledge and equipment. The first aid courses run by St Johns and The Mountain Safety Council are worthwhile. I'd encourage you to attend one. A few hours spent doing these courses provides you with a lifelong skill and could save much suffering.

The first time you come across an accident or emergency it is hard not to be overwhelmed. Your mind goes blank. Panic and confusion set in and the situation rapidly deteriorates. Being prepared in terms of training, knowledge and equipment reduces this chaos and allows you to use the two greatest tools of bush survival — commonsense and calm.

First aid in the bush is not about miraculously healing the seriously injured. It is about doing your best in a bad situation and stabilising the person till help arrives. If the victim doesn't make it don't blame yourself. At least by trying you gave them a chance.

BASIC FIRST AID KIT

I'm often asked by hunters and trampers what they should take with them as a first aid kit. The answer really depends on how far from help you will be, how long and risky your trip is and how confident you are at treatment. Commercially prepared first aid kits are good but are bulky and often contain only dressings. Many of these can be improvised in the bush from clothing, flax etc. The following are two suggested lists that can be added to if you have room. Most items can be bought from a chemist. The drugs you will need to get on prescription, with advice, from your family doctor.

Short trips e.g. 1 to 2 days:

Space blanket

Dressings for cuts / blisters — 2 non-adhesive 75 by 100mm dressings

Tape e.g. Leukoplast®, and Elastoplast® dressing strip

Pain relief — Paracetamol or Aspirin and "Nurofen®" or "Voltaren®"

Anti-histamines e.g. Loratadine®

Obviously if you have an illness such as asthma or diabetes take the relevant medication.

Long trips such as 10 days in the South Island high country or an isolated Stewart Island block:

The same as above, but add extra non-adhesive dressings, tape and elastoplast.

4 crepe bandage 100mm.

Steristrips to close a clean open wound.

Triangular bandage.

Antibiotics — "Augmentin" is a good broad spectrum antibiotic for skin, chest, sinus, throat, dental and urine infections. Erythromycin is an alternative if you are allergic to penicillin. Honey applied to wounds reduces infection. Take some antibiotic eye ointment for conjunctivitis.

Prednisone — This is a useful medicine for severe allergies and bouts of asthma. Both of these are common and can be life-threatening. It is also useful for treating gout. Prednisone is a steroid and should only be used with medical advice. If you do start either prednisone or antibiotics you should consider getting back to medical help as soon as possible.

"Buccastem" and "Diastop" — several guys in close proximity in a grubby backcountry hut often results in a bout of diarrhoea and vomiting.

Sunscreen and insect repellent.

Steroid creams such as hydrocortisone or "betnovate" for sunburn, insect bites etc

Antifungal creams for athlete's foot or jock itch.

If you have a condition such as asthma, angina, diabetes, epilepsy etc carry the appropriate medications and tell your mates what to do should you develop a worsening problem. Get advice from your doctor about what to do in an emergency. If in doubt bail out early and call for help. Take a mountain radio.

MAJOR TRAUMA

2005 was a bad year for hunting accidents. One of our worst nightmares is to have to deal with major injuries in the bush, either from a fall, or worse a gunshot wound.

The following are some suggestions on when to call for help and things you could do while waiting for evacuation.

(a)

Placing a person in the recovery position.

(b)

(c)

When faced with an accident an automatic reaction is to rush in and help. Too much haste leads to confusion and will make you ineffective or even dangerous. Take a few moments to calmly assess the situation, especially in relation to your own safety.

If you are unlucky enough to come across someone who is unconscious, call for help and do an ABC (airway, breathing, circulation) assessment. A full description of CPR is beyond the scope of this article and should be covered in a first aid course. Ensure the airway is open and clear the mouth of blood clots, vomit etc without moving the neck if there might be a spinal injury. Check for breathing and if none start mouth to mouth resuscitation. After a couple of breaths, check for a pulse in the neck beside the Adams apple. When the person is very cold or very ill, the pulse can be quite slow and subtle. If, after a short search, you can't find a pulse start cardiac compressions. Once they are breathing independently put them in the recovery position.

Opening the airway – head tilt chin lift method

If the patient has fainted, they should revive within 1 minute.

Temporary improvised treatment for shock or faint.

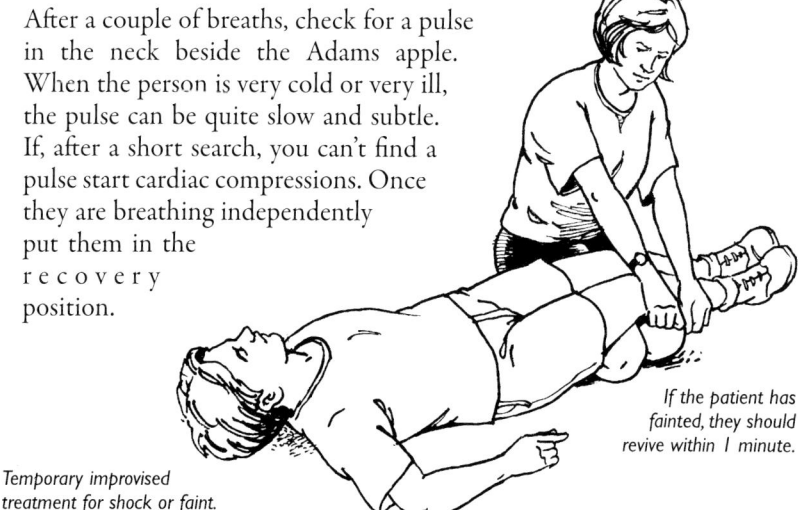

The next important consideration is to stop bleeding. This is best done by direct pressure on the wound for 5–15 minutes. If direct pressure is not stopping the bleeding, put firm pressure on the artery in the groin or armpit. Only as a last resort use a tourniquet. If the person is shocked, i.e. pale / sweaty with a rapid weak pulse, lift the legs up and head down. If a foreign body, e.g. a branch is sticking out of the wound, do not remove it.

Don't assume that the obvious injury is the only one. Either ask the person or examine them thoroughly.

Severely injured people often rapidly get cold. Try to keep them off the ground using a sleeping mat and cover them with a space blanket.

"Tough" guys in the bush will often try to make light of their injuries. Don't believe them.

If you are treating someone with a major injury and help is near don't give them anything to eat or drink as they are likely to need surgery.

When there is a near drowning, and the person seems to have recovered, they should be evacuated as they can deteriorate up to 48 hours later.

Anyone who has been unconscious for whatever reason should be evacuated.

While waiting for help reassess the person regularly as their condition may change rapidly.

Severe head injury

Remember that neck injuries often go with head injuries. If the person is disorientated, complains of nausea, has a loss of memory of the accident and is unsteady, they have moderate to severe concussion and should be seen by a doctor as soon as possible. If they have any of the following signs they need to be evacuated urgently:

1] Prolonged loss of consciousness of more than 5 minutes

2] Increasing headache or nausea

3] Convulsion

4] Weak slow pulse
5] Unequal pupils
6] Developing numbness, weakness in any part of the body or becoming less conscious.

A change in symptoms suggests a bleed in the skull cavity and may occur many hours after the accident. A head injury patient is often drowsy. It is OK to let them sleep but wake them every 15 to 30 minutes to check their level of consciousness is not deteriorating.

Spinal injury

Always assume a spinal injury if the person is unconscious or if they complain of back / neck pain or numbness / tingling / weakness anywhere. Do not

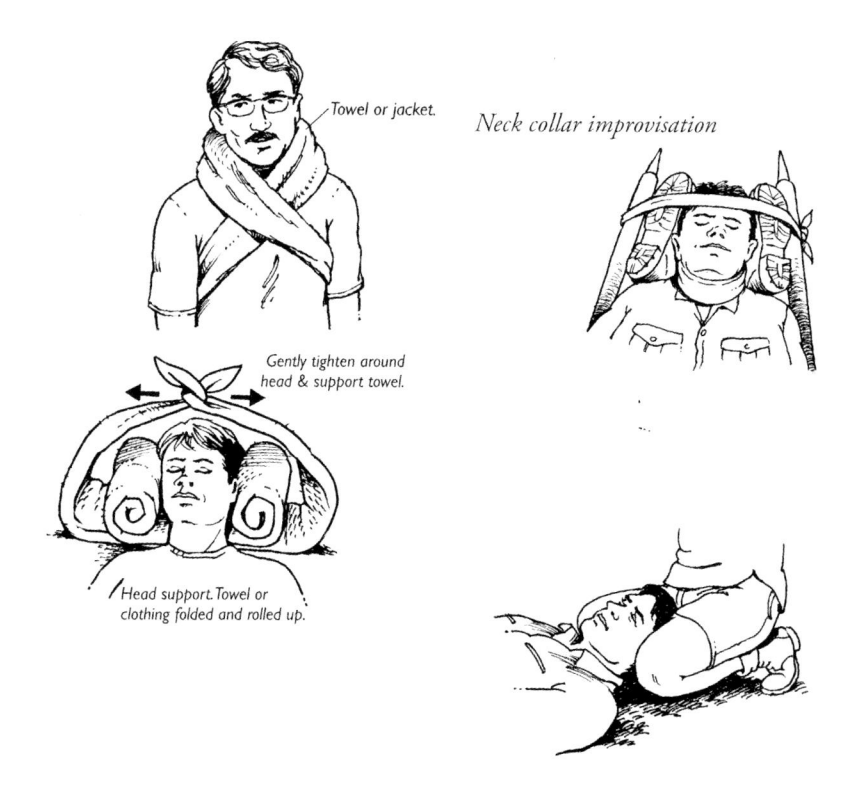

Towel or jacket.

Neck collar improvisation

Gently tighten around head & support towel.

Head support. Towel or clothing folded and rolled up.

move them unless absolutely necessary and then only with the spine well supported. A rolled up jacket or strip of closed cell foam mattress wrapped firmly around the neck will help. Because there will be a greatly increased risk of hypothermia, keep them dry and warm until help arrives.

Chest injuries

A pneumothorax (burst lung) should be suspected in all cases of fractured ribs, especially if there are multiple fractures, if the person is short of breath, develops a cough, shoulder pain or blood stained sputum. It can be accompanied by a lot of blood loss into the chest.

When 2 or more ribs are broken in 2 places, it creates a segment of the chest that moves independently from the rest of the chest, a "flail segment". It is very painful and prevents the lungs from inflating properly, causing severe respiratory distress. Tape a large pad firmly into the flail segment.

Anyone injured like this except for simple, uncomplicated fracture ribs should be evacuated.

Open chest wounds such as gunshot wounds should be sealed immediately with plastic and taped on 3 sides only. (Don't use glad wrap as it will get sucked into the wound). This allows air to get out of the chest but not be sucked in. Remember the exit wound.

The best position for a conscious person with breathing difficulties is sitting semi-upright leaning towards the injured side. Keep them as quiet as possible.

Abdominal injuries: A huge amount of blood can be lost quickly into the abdomen from a ruptured liver, spleen or kidney, usually from a fall onto a rock or branch. Anyone with a significant blow to the abdomen or pelvis, especially if they develop increasing pain or a tense swollen abdomen, should be evacuated as

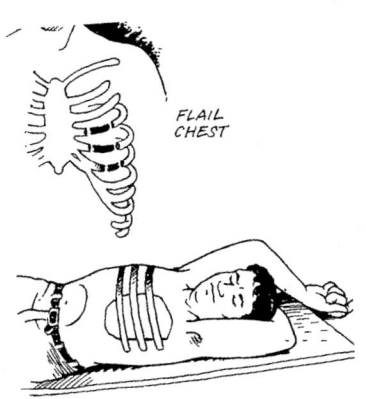

Open chest injury.
Improvising a one-way air valve.

Open chest injury. Improvising a one-way air valve

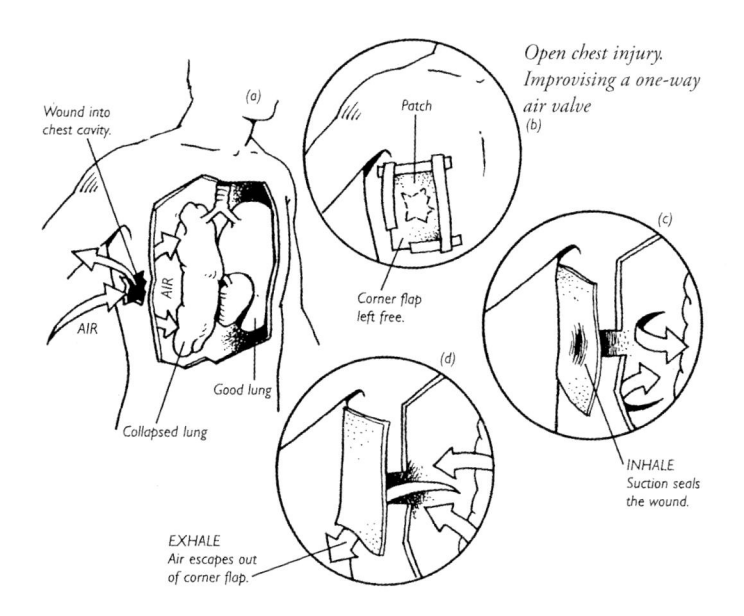

soon as possible. The liver is tucked under the lower ribs on the right and the spleen on the left, so they can be involved if there is a chest injury. Keep the patient lying quietly with the legs raised. If they are unconscious, put them in the recovery position.

Gun shot wounds to the abdomen often have gut protruding. Don't push it back in. Just cover it with a clean damp cloth or dressing while waiting for help.

Major fractures: One of the most important fractures is the femur or thigh bone. This can result in enough blood loss into the thigh to cause shock. To prevent this, tie the two feet and legs together firmly, with a padded branch in between them, to keep the legs straight and prevent the affected one from shortening. This also helps to minimise the pain.

If there is exposed bone, don't try to push it back in or straighten the limb. The only time you should try to straighten a fracture is if the circulation is severely affected, i.e. no pulse and a cold white limb. Just splint it and cover the exposed bone with a clean damp cloth till help arrives. Splinting simply involves tying or taping the limb in several places to a rigid object, e.g. a branch, to prevent movement and so control pain and prevent further damage. Splints should include the joints above and below the fracture. Closed cell foam sleeping mats can be wrapped around the fractured limb and make excellent splints. Internal frame packs often have flexible aluminum stays that can be moulded and used as splints. Use plenty of packing and keep an eye on the pulses and colour of the limb.

Fractures of the arm, once splinted, are usually best kept in a sling or pin the sleeve to the inside of a jacket. If the elbow is broken, keep the arm straight. Remove any rings.

Don't try to put back in place a dislocated joint like a shoulder. You never know if it is also fractured.

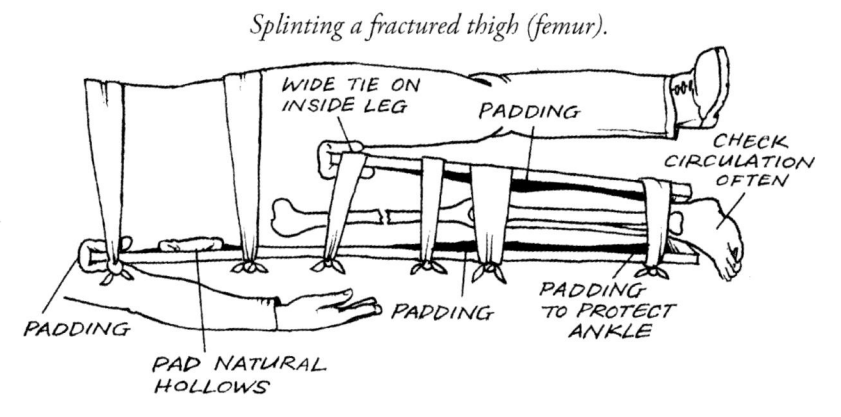

Splinting a fractured thigh (femur).

WOUND CARE

Probably the most common bush injury would be a laceration or cut. Most of these can be managed with a simple first aid kit. There are, however, some important complications such as infection, blood loss and tendon or nerve damage that need to be considered.

The first priority is to stop the bleeding. This is best done with firm pressure for 5–15 minutes. Don't use a tourniquet unless absolutely necessary. If there is a large foreign body like a branch in the wound, don't remove it. Simply apply pressure around it by squeezing the edges of the wound together. If the bleeding is arterial or the wound very large, apply a firm compression bandage, splint and elevate the limb while waiting for help.

Less serious wounds where the bleeding has been controlled can now be cleaned. Pour clean water or preferably salt water (2tsp salt to 1L water) over the wound to wash out leaves and obvious dirt. Honey applied to the wound reduces infection and promotes healing.

Wounds sustained in the bush often get infected especially when they are big, dirty or have foreign material embedded in them. Bites almost always get infected, as do wounds that extend into a joint. The person will need antibiotics and should get out of the bush as soon as possible.

Tendon and nerve damage are common with deep lacerations. The sooner they are fixed surgically the more chance of success so if you suspect this get help as soon as possible. For example, a minor cut to the side of a finger can make the tip of that finger numb; quite debilitating in the long term, especially if it is your trigger finger! Likewise, a cut to the back of the hand can sever a tendon preventing a finger from straightening.

Wound dressings can be improvised in the bush from clothing or flax etc. The first layer, however, should be a sterile, non adhesive commercial dressing, available from a chemist. Dressings should be changed daily. Steristrips or any tape can be used to close wounds that are small and clean.

Tetanus still affects a few people in NZ every year. It is a nasty, potentially fatal illness that tends to get in through dirty wounds. Make sure your booster vaccination is up to date.

If you are treating someone with a laceration, try to minimise contact with their blood. Although HIV is not yet common in NZ, Hepatitis B and C are and are transmitted through infected body fluids.

Crush injuries such as those sustained from a rockslide or fallen tree, cause massive tissue damage and need evacuation. Don't assume it is just bruising.

Blisters: Prevention is better than cure. Break in a new pair of boots before a big trip and ensure they fit well. Wear a thin, liner sock under heavier ones. Friction will occur between the socks instead of between the sock and skin. Tape any possible friction spots and keep the laces tight. Don't keep going in wet socks if blisters are likely and if you do feel a blister starting cover it with a small dressing taped down firmly. A large fluid-filled blister is best drained and then covered.

SOFT TISSUE INJURIES

I often hear people describe twisting an ankle in the bush and simply tightening their boot laces and walking out, with great difficulty. This is usually quite reasonable if it is a simple sprain, but it is often hard to decide if there is an underlying fracture. A patient of mine once walked for three hours on a so called sprained ankle, only to find the resultant swelling in a tight boot almost cut the circulation. The boot had to be cut off. He had a badly fractured ankle! If in doubt, treat the injury as a fracture, especially if the tenderness is over the prominent bony parts on either side of the ankle. Try not to walk on these injuries. Call for help.

The immediate treatment in the bush for a sprain is RICE — Rest. Ice or anything cold, such as dipping the affected part in a cold stream as often as possible. Compression with a bandage is difficult to do adequately in the bush. Elevate the limb above the level of your heart.

Using pain relief is reasonable, but beware of hiding a serious injury so that you can carry on hunting.

Strains occur when muscle is torn by excessive force. The treatment (RICE) is the same. Don't rub the affected part.

Tendonitis: Tendons can get inflamed if they are overused or suddenly used in a different way. If lower limb tendonitis develops, have your boots reassessed to see if they suit your foot shape. You may need a heel raise for Achilles tendonitis, for example. Podiatrists and physiotherapists will advise you on this.

Cramp: The most common causes of this are being too cold, dehydrated or not taking adequate salt. Treat by stretching and rubbing the affected part.

Trench foot: Many days of constant cold wet feet can produce this condition, leading to nerve and blood vessel damage. The skin becomes red, swollen, mottled and numb. After a few more days the skin ulcerates and is painful. Treat this as you would frostbite by keeping the area dry, warm and minimising walking.

BURNS

Most of us who have cooked over open fires or used camp stoves will have suffered at least one burn. Painful and apt to provoke some colourful language.

Burns must be taken very seriously and the person evacuated if they involve the face, hands, feet or genitals or if they involve over 10% of the body surface. The palm of one hand is about 1%. Deep burns will be relatively pain free as the nerves are dead. They will look pale and charred. Superficial burns will be painful, red and blistered.

Large burns, even if superficial, will cause a lot of fluid loss and lead to potentially life-threatening shock. Subsequent infection is common.

Treatment: Remove anything in contact with the person that might retain heat, including clothing and jewellery. Run cold water over the burn for 10 minutes, then cover with a clean damp cloth to help relieve the pain. Elevate the limb.

If the burn is large, give frequent sips of fluid to prevent dehydration and lessen shock. Even if the burn is only on the legs, remove rings from fingers as there may be generalised swelling. Blisters can be very large and should not be broken unless infected.

Superficial burns of less than 5% body surface can be managed like any other wound with hygienic non-adhesive dressings.

Inhalation burns, caused by breathing in burning gases or very hot air need urgent evacuation even though they may seem OK initially. The airway is likely to swell later.

Remember, severe sunburn can cause shock if a large enough area is affected.

HYPOTHERMIA

One of the main dangers to face a hunter in the NZ bush throughout the year is hypothermia. Put simply, the three main environmental causes of hypothermia are wind, wet and cold. The body can handle one of these, but

A happy Michael Edwards with his first deer, a Red spiker that needed to be culled due to the poor quality of its head. Shooting the animal is one thing, carrying it out and preparing it for the table is another!

Roger Stokes with a big Red – Mt Aspiring National Park. (Photo: Simon Gibson)

If your rifle wasn't correctly sighted in, would you be certain of connecting with these Red deer?

two or three elements combined have a rapid and dangerous effect. Water conducts heat 23 times faster than air, so it's not hard to imagine the effects of cold rain or sweat. At 0°C a breeze strong enough to move small branches will produce a wind chill factor of about -13! Approximately 70% of heat loss in a sensibly clothed individual occurs through the head and neck by radiation and evaporation, so wearing a hat has the same effect as putting the lid on a billy — it helps it to boil! Multi-layered, synthetic windproof clothing (not cotton) is best.

Hypothermia develops when core temperature drops below 35°C (normal 37°C). This is hard to measure, so be aware of the danger and look for the following symptoms:

Mild (core temp 33–35°C): cold extremities, shivering, fast heart rate and breathing, frequent urination and slight inco-ordination.

Moderate (31–33°C): clumsy, tired, less shivering, weak, drowsy, slurred speech, poor judgment, apathy.

Severe (<31°C): no shivering, muscle stiffness, inappropriate behaviour, slow weak pulse, reduced consciousness, dangerous heart rhythms. Appears dead at <28°C.

The person may only complain of feeling tired not cold.

Exhaustion and inadequate food intake prevent shivering (the body's way of generating heat) and so speeds the process up, as does dehydration and too much handling or rubbing.

Treatment:

Call for help early. Remove the person from cold, wet or windy conditions with shelter and dry clothes. If not possible, use a big plastic bag from the neck down, then a warm dry jacket then another plastic bag on top. Don't forget a warm dry hat. Space blankets are great and should be carried by everyone. Unless you are dealing with mild hypothermia, avoid active re-warming, such as body-to-body contact etc, as this only draws warm blood from the core to the cold skin and further cools it. Minimal _gentle_ handling is important in preventing dangerous heart rhythms. Warm sweet drinks are good so long as the person can swallow without choking but please avoid alcohol. It is fatal. Rewarming can take many hours.

Don't give up trying to revive someone even though they may appear dead.

HYPERTHERMIA (overheating)

The human body has an amazing ability to exercise in a wide range of environmental extremes while keeping a core temperature of about 37°C. Far better than most man-made machines. Everything has its limits, however, and exercise in hot weather can have its dangers.

Heat stroke, an often fatal condition, is usually the domain of the elite endurance athlete, but heat exhaustion is probably quite common in hunters and trampers. This latter occurs when the core body temperature rises to about 39°C. In practical terms, it is hard to measure core temperature in the bush, so beware of symptoms that include thirst, muscle cramps, dizziness, weakness, nausea and headache. If it progresses to heat stroke, the person may become confused, irrational, aggressive, stop sweating and go unconscious as the temperature reaches 41°C.

It may seem obvious that the cause of heat exhaustion is excessive exercise (heat production) in hot humid weather (poor heat loss) but there are other factors. Certain individuals are at greater risk, including those who are unfit, obese, very young or old, not used to the heat or who are not drinking enough. Certain blood pressure medications also predispose to heat stress. Drinking water is adequate if you exercise in the heat for up to 1 hour, but after that watered-down fruit juice or electrolyte drinks are best at a rate of 1 litre per hour. They are absorbed 30% faster. Rehydration fluids can be made up from either 50/50 water / fruit juice or 1 tsp sugar or honey and 1 pinch salt to 1 mug of water.

One of the main risks is exercising while you have an infection. Many people still believe the old wives tale that the best treatment for a cold or flu is to "sweat it out" by exercising. This is asking for trouble, and not just from heat stroke. A good rule with infections is the "neck rule". If you have an infection above the neck, such as a runny nose or minor sore throat, exercise is fine. If you have any symptoms below the neck, such as a fever or cough, do not exercise strenuously, even in cool weather.

The risk of heat exhaustion also depends on the humidity and wind speed. Hot, humid and still weather limits the ability to effectively sweat. Appropriate clothing is important.

The treatment for heat exhaustion is to rest in the shade, drink plenty, remove excess clothing and sponge the head and neck with cool water. Put the person in the recovery position, take off clothing and sponge the bare skin with cool water. Arrange an urgent evacuation.

FROSTBITE

I once knew a very successful Sika hunter who prided himself in stalking very quietly because he never wore boots or shoes while actively hunting. After one cold winter morning hunt and a painful toe that later turned black, he changed his mind!

Frostbite mainly affects those bits that stick out, like the nose, ears, toes and fingers. The person may be unaware it is happening as the surface layers of tissue freeze becoming numb and pale. As the deeper layers become frozen, the area feels hard. Frostbite is more common and severe if the area is wet, or if the body core is already cold (hypothermic). As the frostbitten part thaws, it may become painful, swollen, red and blistered. Severe frostbite will turn black or gangrenous.

Apart from adequate clothing and keeping dry, the best way to prevent frostbite is to keep your core body temperature normal.

Treatment:

It is better to leave a frostbitten area frozen rather than thaw it and have it refreeze. So once thawed, pay special attention to keeping the area warm. Do not rub frostbite or walk on a frostbitten foot, as the tissue damage will be vastly increased. Re-warm the area by putting it next to another warm part of the body, for example, fingers placed in the armpit or a warm hand held over a frostbitten ear.

If you are trying to re-warm frozen toes or fingers, be careful not to burn them as they will be numb. If you are using warm water, start with lukewarm water and raise the temperature slowly. This will be a painful process, so after thawing keep the part elevated and give pain relief, preferably aspirin.

Chapter 8   WHEN YOU GET LOST!

Thanks to Dave Comber who contributed this section. Dave has been involved in Search and Rescue for over forty years and has been awarded the New Zealand Land SAR service award in recognition of his contribution on both a national and local level. His comments come from a long experience.

SOME GOOD ADVICE ON WHAT TO DO IF YOU GET LOST OR IN TROUBLE

There is an old saying that there are only two types of hunters: those who have spent a night out and those who are going to spend a night out. Although the advent of the GPS has decreased dramatically the number of SAR callouts for lost hunters, there will still be the odd occasion when something goes wrong and someone either gets hopelessly lost or into a difficult situation.

It is a generally accepted fact that the majority of people who get lost very quickly become incapable of rational thought. These people often make a quite minor incident into a potentially life-threatening one by doing silly things, often in a panic. On the other hand, there are incredible stories of people surviving seemingly impossible odds in really bad situations. The secret seems to be keeping your head and staying calm.

Some time ago I was watching a documentary on survival. In it a mnemonic was advocated, which I thought brilliant in both its simplicity and applicability to our typical SAR scenario in the New Zealand bush and high country. The mnemonic is "STOP" and it goes like this:

Stop

If you are unsure of your position, or are involved in an incident, the first thing to do is stop and calm down. If you smoke — light up. Have a muesli bar or something and force yourself to start thinking straight. Your worst enemy in the New Zealand bush is simply your own confusion or fears.

Take Stock

Assess your situation and equipment. What is the weather like and what is the forecast? How long is it before dark? How well are you clothed for the conditions? What gear and food have you got on you? Are you hurt or exhausted? When did you last eat or drink? What is the country like you are in? Do you need to move or is it dry and warm where you are? Are you close to water? Does anyone know where you are? When would you expect an alarm to be raised?

Orientate Yourself

Get your map and compass out (I would like to think you have these with you) and your GPS, if you have one. Work out your position even if it is only approximate. You can get pretty close by marking where you were last sure of your position on the map and projecting an approximate direction and distance (base on maximum 500m/hour if hunting) travelled from there. Note major features and obstacles in your vicinity.

Plan

Now that you are thinking straight, have done an inventory of your situation and know where you are, you are in a position to make a plan. Consider how far you will need to travel, how long you have been overdue etc. It may be that your plan is simply to stay put, make yourself as comfortable and visible as possible, then wait for SAR to turn up.

Please bear in mind that if you have spent a night out, and been reported overdue by your party, SAR will generally be mobilised by early afternoon. If you are not certain of making it back to camp by the end of the day, please stop moving and do what you can to make yourself visible from the air. If you have come across a hut or bivvy, do not leave it, as one of our first actions is to use a local helicopter operator to check out all the huts and bivvies in the area. In the bush it is very difficult to locate a person who is moving.

Author's note: The New Mountain Safety Council have some excellent resources available on safety in the mountains that are well worth checking out. Their website is mountainsafety.org.nz

Also check out the website of the New Zealand Search and Rescue Council,

www.beacons.org.nz or freephone 0800 406 111 for information on Emergency Locator Beacons. It may be cheap insurance to carry one if you are venturing into difficult terrain.

Keep our environment clean and tidy — remove your rubbish.

PART TWO

FROM THE KILL TO THE CARRY

- § Stalking tips
- § Shoot to kill
- § Field butchery and hygiene issues
- § How to carry your animal out whole
- § In camp
- § Keeping your skins
- § If you shoot a trophy

A deer is not worth the life of your mate.

Chapter 9   STALKING TIPS

Here are some basic starters:

» Dawn and dusk are generally the best times to hunt deer, although in areas where there is little or no helicopter activity you may find deer out at any time. With Sika in the roar you often get onto stags around midday.

» Hunt with the wind in your face if at all possible. If you have ever seen the disgusted look on the face of an animal that has just scented you, you will know why! Remember too that the wind may eddy back over ridges and in such cases can be deceiving. Watch the low-flying cloud in the wind and you will see what I mean.

» In the morning the warm air rises so it tends to drift up the valley, whereas in the evening as the temperature drops the wind drifts down the valley. Your smell goes with it.

» Wear lightweight boots or footwear when bush stalking, not great heavy clunkers!

» Try to make as little noise as possible. Make sure you have nothing in your gear that rattles or makes noise and wear clothing that is quiet. For example, remove your quick release sling swivels when you hit the bush – they are noisy!

» Hunt river flats, clearings or the bush edge at dawn and dusk, when the deer are heading out to feed or returning to cover from feeding areas. Take your time when looking at clearings as there may well be a feeding deer hidden behind a bush or in a dip. You are more likely to get Rusa out on sunny faces at about 10 am. All warm blooded animals like the sun so remember that when you're looking for likely places. Also remember that deer tend to begin moving later in the afternoon as they become hungry.

» Make sure if you're hunting flats or the bush edge that you are up and away well before dawn. I've known hunters to head out for these regions about morning tea and wonder why all they see is old sign!

» Bush stalking can be productive for most of the day, especially during the roar and through the early part of the winter.

» A great time to hunt is after rain and especially on days with intermittent showers and nice sunny spells.

» It is better to stay higher if possible as you have a better vantage point and it is easier looking down, rather than up.

» Spend lots of time looking rather than walking, even in the bush and especially when you find an area with a lot of sign. A good pair of binoculars gives you a great advantage if you are in more open country.

» Stay off ridge lines if possible as your silhouette and movement may alert any game.

» When you come to a ridge, even in the bush, take care as you stalk over it. It often pays to pause and look carefully before you move.

» When you think you may be onto an animal go really slowly. Stop, take a slow step, stop again and look. Don't be in a hurry.

» If you spot an animal and you need to move, do so when it has its head down.

» Plan where you will hunt, both before you go out for the day and in the immediate i.e. when you are in the bush don't just wander around in the hope that you'll see something. Think about which ridge you will go up and how you'll stalk it and where you'll stop. Good hunters are thinking hunters.

» If you are going into a new area, get a good map and blow up on a photocopier the immediate area you will be hunting. Mark on that the grid references for longitude and latitude, so you can find your way with a GPS. Laminate your map so it is usable in all weather.

» Don't camp right in the middle of a good area. That's a great giveaway to deer, except for Whitetail who seem to persist in hanging around camps for some obscure reason.

» Remember deer are warm blooded animals and in colder times will generally be found in areas facing north where they get the sun.

» If it's foggy, smile – the deer will think it's ok to stay out longer. For some reason fog seems to give them a false sense of security, so don't stay in the hut – get out and hunt!

» Wet weather doesn't always mean the hunting is no good, so don your wet weather gear and have a look. Red deer seem to worry less about the wet than do Sika, and we used to shoot a lot of Reds in the wet when meat hunting.

» Don't be fooled – the best hunting is often not two days' walk away or a helicopter flight away into the hills. It can be quite close at hand.

» If you have to talk to a mate, keep the volume of your voices as low as possible. It is amazing how far the human voice carries in the wild and deer do have a better sense of hearing than we do.

» If you have roared at a stag make sure you wait for a decent length of time. As a restless hunter I can speak from experience of stuffing up many an animal because I moved away too soon.

» You will find deer in different places at different times of the year. Obviously the roar is a premium time, but during March, with Sika in particular, you may find them right out in the open. From mid January to the end of February Reds seem to disappear to cooler regions, only to reappear in March. We found also that the stags would come right down on the river flats during the roar. May too is often a good time to hunt Reds and Sika as they feed up before winter. In July, August and early September you'll find animals harder to find as their metabolism slows down with the cold of winter and they move around less. In August, September and October with all the new grass, you'll wonder where they all came from.

» Don't neglect to have a look at clearings during the day, especially when hunting Sika. One of the best Sika hunters I know sees a good number of animals on clearings from about 10.30 on until after midday.

» Successful hunters generally know their favourite hunting areas intimately. Find a good area and then get to know it well. Learn where the clearings are, observe the direction of the prevailing wind, note the best places to approach possible hot spots from, the best access ridges and other key features such as river flats and benches that may be good areas in the roar.

» When you are hunting, NEVER assume anything! Never assume that because you cannot see anything, there is nothing there! Never assume that because you cannot see them, they cannot see you! Never assume that the noise you hear or the movement you see is a deer, just because it sounds and looks like a deer - it may be your mate who shouldn't be there!

» A good safety tip: if you can identify the sex of an animal, then it surely is a deer!

» Be patient and persist in your hunting. The best of us go through dry patches when we don't seem to get onto anything. You never know what's around the next bend or over the next ridge, or on the scene the next day! Deer are where you find them! Remember the worst day's hunting is better than any day at work, and the testing times build character. Read as much as you can and watch quality videos or DVDs from people like Neil Philpott, Dawson Bliss and the Graff brothers. If you are still having no success at all, talk to someone who is an experienced hunter or go out with a guide for a weekend. Join a hunting club. If you don't ask, you won't receive.

Commonsense at all times.

Chapter 10 # SHOOT TO KILL

What to shoot?

The best animals for the dinner table are the young ones. Use a bit of discretion though when shooting for meat. If you see a young stag in velvet that has a potential trophy class head, leave it and find something else. On the other hand, if you find an animal like the one depicted earlier in the book that will never grow a good set of antlers, and in fact if left may pass on bad genes, knock it over. You are doing the cause a favour. I believe the attitude of many New Zealand hunters has to change. Too many guys tell themselves, "If I don't shoot it, someone else will". Well, maybe they will, but maybe they won't, and maybe if an increasing number of us hunt with an eye to the future, we will have better heads to shoot. Just think — that young stag you or someone else let go, may grow up to be the fantastic trophy you shoot in four years' time!!! Short-term pain for long-term gain.

Placement of your shot

The placement of your shot is critical. Shoot a deer in the chest cavity, hit a vital organ and the animal should drop within a short distance. Of course the tenacity of individual animals varies and some species are a little harder to drop than others, but the correct placement of your shot with the right bullet will generally do the trick. Most modern game bullets are fine and over the years I've tried a good number of them as well as some homemade creations. They all generally work well, but the key is placement of your shot. I knew one ex-culler who shot only solid point projectiles from his .308 and he swore by them. Not my ideal, as solid projectiles are designed to completely penetrate and so expend much of their energy on the landscape. However, he was a good shot and that helped no end. From time to time I hear of hunters complaining of such and such a projectile, but I believe the problem is generally with the hunter. They either miss or hit an animal in the wrong place and put the blame elsewhere. It always makes them look better of course.

A shot in the chest cavity with the right bullet will generally kill an animal quickly. Good advice is to aim to break the shoulder on the other side of the animal. If a deer is broadside on, I generally follow up the front leg until about halfway up the chest cavity and then touch off.

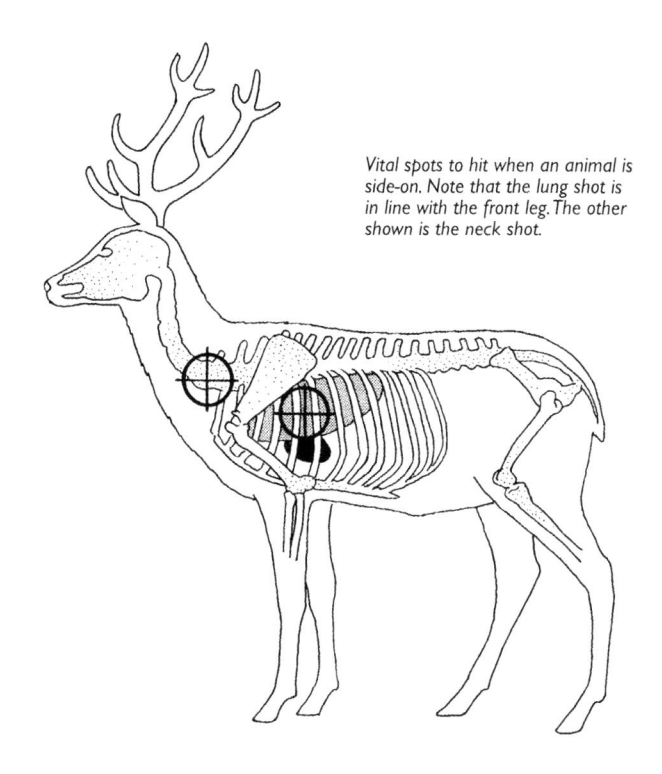

Vital spots to hit when an animal is side-on. Note that the lung shot is in line with the front leg. The other shown is the neck shot.

Diagram used by permission of Mountain Safety Council.

Note there is very little in the area behind the rib cage for a bullet to open up on and nothing vital — not a good place for a shot. It is also easy to miss the spine. A shot in the hindquarters will drop an animal especially if it hits bone, but it will significantly damage the meat. The neck shot is a good option if the animal is close and if you can shoot straight! One advantage of the neck shot is minimal meat damage. Many of the deer we shot while meat hunting were shot in the neck for that reason. Also neck-shot deer generally don't run away! Exception here is with Sambar and big stags which can have huge neck muscles. A fellow Taupo hunter recently fired two rounds from a .303 into the neck of a wounded Sambar stag from close range with no effect! A shot into the chest finally did the trick.

Chapter 11 FIELD BUTCHERY AND HYGIENE ISSUES

YOU'VE SHOT IT... WHAT NOW?

Check to make sure it's dead! If it's a stag with antlers, approach from behind and give it a dig in the backside, with your rifle ready if you have any doubts. The best thing to do if it's still quite conscious is to shoot again, remembering that antlers can be a lethal weapon. "Dead" stags have been known to get up and run away. Recently I shot a stag in the head and he appeared to be inert and virtually dead, so I stuck my knife into his chest where I knew his heart would be. At that he whipped his antlers around, catching me a good blow on my leg and my knife went flying. It could have been quite serious and I was a bit slack, to be honest!

Tim with two Sika spikers he shot for meat, right under the nose of his father! Now the fun begins with the dressing out and carry back home.

When you know the animal is quite dead, it's time to begin to dress it out. As you do so, check to see it's in good condition. When you gut it, take particular notice of the liver. If it's covered with white splotches and otherwise looks odd, get it checked out. We can get a bit paranoiac about this sort of thing as a result of misinformation from the media and some government bureaucrats who only ever see the inside of a stuffy little office, but like to think they are making decisions of earth-shattering importance. In actual fact I've never shot a deer that I would consider had a death-inviting disease. I did attempt to dress a hind my son shot one time and ended up chucking it all out, because I think she was the last of the original Sika still alive from the first release. She was so old she should have received a telegram from the Queen. Instead she had the pleasure of meeting my son!

As a sideline, you can tell the relative age of a deer by the colour of its bones. A young animal has an almost purplish tinge, whereas an adult animal in its prime has white coloured bone. You'll know a grandma or grandad by a yellowish colour — can't miss it as it is a yucky pale colour. In this case the meat, if edible, is probably best for sausages.

SOME KEY THINGS TO NOTE REGARDING HYGIENE

The following comments apply particularly to an animal you wish to carry out <u>whole</u>, but the basic principles of hygiene remain the same regardless of whether you bone an animal out in the field or process it at home.

1] In terms of hygiene, the goal is to keep your meat as CLEAN as possible. If you are after meat, pretend you are Daniel Boone and try and neck shoot the animal.

2] Wherever meat is cut, bacteria enters — the fewer cuts the better. That's why in some respects it's better to carry the animal out whole. In fact if you choose to butcher the whole animal at home you will increase significantly your chances of keeping the meat clean.

3] If you have to gut the deer, try and avoid cutting open the gut bag or stomach if at all possible. Bacteria from the gut will contaminate the meat and possibly make it spoil more quickly.

4] Don't open the neck right up until you are ready to bone out the meat. Again this allows bacteria in.

Guess how far away this 14 point Red stag is. Wouldn't you feel much more confident with a range finder?

The author with one of the best Rusa shot in New Zealand in the last thirty years. DS 185.

If you were hunting just for meat, a neck shot would be ideal to secure this Red hind. A bum shot could wreck too much meat.

Fallow venison is tasty and this shot is as easy as you can expect. A good option would be to sit down and drop it with a shot through the base of the neck. Better to aim there than at the neck if you are not too confident, as the neck on a Fallow deer is a small target.

5] Wipe any dirt off the meat rather than splashing water on it. You may think water is clean! Ever had a look at it through a microscope? It's full of nasty little bacteria. Dirt, likewise, has a good few bugs! You may think that what you don't see won't hurt you. Food poisoning ain't fun!

6] If an animal is gut-shot, clean it up as best as you can. Wipe it out with clumps of grass if necessary. You'll notice a gut-shot deer attracts more flies too — more dirt, more bacteria, more flies! What an incentive to hone up your shooting skills and make sure you shoot the deer in the right place!

7] After gutting the animal, drain as much of the liquid from inside the chest and stomach cavity as possible. Just lift it up and drain it out the back end.

8] Keep the animal or the meat cool. Heat will make it spoil more quickly, sometimes within a few hours. So don't leave it in the sun and don't leave it in the boot of your car with gear all over it, sitting outside the pub in the sun for a few hours while you celebrate. While you are getting high something else may be too, and you may find your celebrations are a little premature!

9] A final suggestion to help keep your meat clean: some hunters carry a lightweight block and tackle set in their day bag so they can hang a deer up from a branch after gutting it, thus making it easier to butcher in the field and to keep the meat away from dirt and leaves. Not a bad idea, because you inevitably get meat somewhat dirty if you try and butcher it on the ground. Even with the best intentions in the world it still seems to attract leaves, grass and other bits and pieces.

TWO CHOICES NOW:

Option 1: Carry out the hindquarters, back steaks and maybe some shoulder meat. **Or Option 2:** Carry it out whole. To do this you will need to gut the animal — see later.

LET'S EXPLORE OPTION 1

Again you have two choices as to how you take your hindquarters out :

a]   Carry out the hindquarters whole, or, b] bone the meat out.

With either of these choices you will not need to gut the animal or remove its head. However, if you want the undercut steaks you will need to remove the gut first. The undercut steaks are found inside the rib cavity at the rear of the backbone, immediately in front of the hindquarters. They are probably the most tender venison you will eat and on a larger animal are definitely worth taking.

To carry out the hindquarters and back steaks without boning the meat out, follow this procedure:

- Roll the deer over onto its belly and run your knife under the skin, sharp side up, down the line of the back bone, from in front of the back legs to the shoulders.

- Then run your knife down the shoulder, halfway to the bottom of the chest and then in a straight line back to the hindquarters.

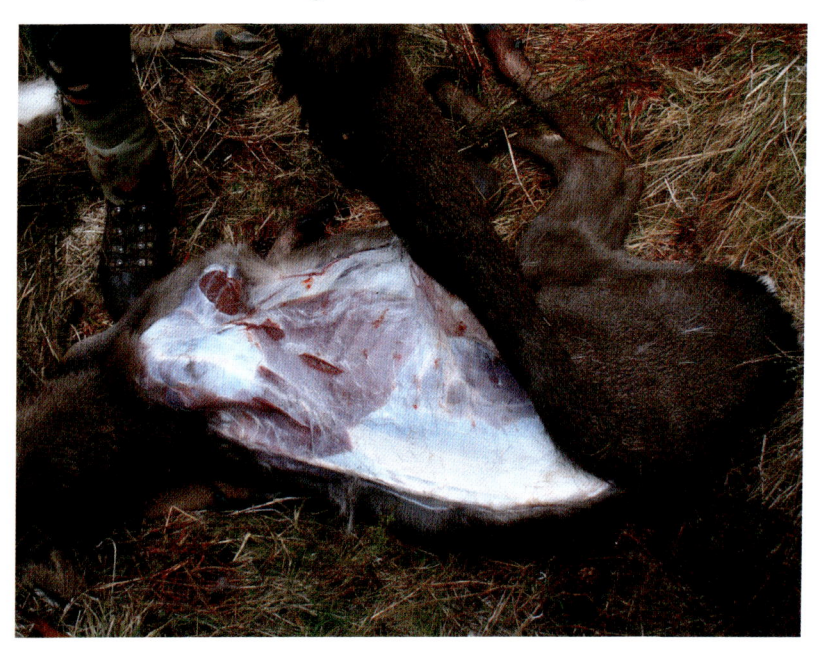

- Peel the skin back on one side, and at this stage you can remove the back steaks on that side. It's easy to do — run your knife down the relevant side of the backbone from the hindquarters to the front shoulder. You can cut virtually right up to the neck, especially if you cut away the front shoulder. Then run your knife parallel to the rib cage and the back steak should just peel off. You may or may not want the front shoulder. Larger deer may have good shoulder meat that you can bone out and keep for small goods.

- Place the back steaks and any other meat you have removed in a suitable muslin bag or an old pillow case you purloined when your wife wasn't looking. Strictly speaking you shouldn't use plastic bags for the meat while it is still warm, but I do when necessary and find the meat stays ok as long is it is not left in them for too long in warm conditions.

- Now do the same on the other side.

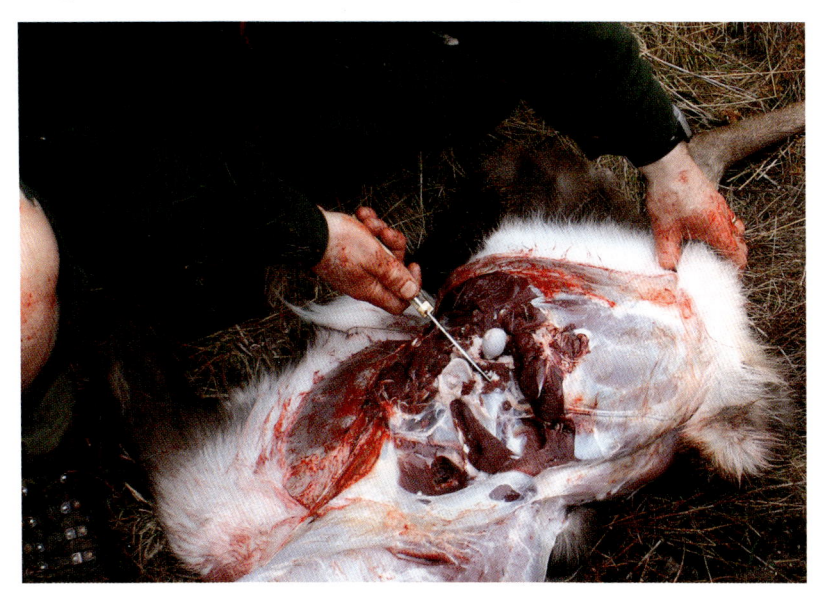

- Once the back steaks are removed, roll the deer over on its back and at this stage you need to remove a hind leg, while keeping the skin attached to it. Push the legs apart and, at the base of the hind leg, cut through to the ball joint and then carefully remove the leg and begin to remove the pelvis from the skin. Repeat for the other leg. You will now have the two hindquarters attached with the skin between them, but with the pelvis removed. The reason for removing the pelvis is to reduce the weight you have to carry. You do lose a bit of meat, but I don't consider that an issue. On a smaller deer you may find there is little meat left behind, but on a larger deer it may well be worth bringing it out. See the end of this section.

- Now before you cut the legs of the deer off at the joint, slit the skin between the tendon and the leg and then cut the tendon about 8–10cm above the joint.

- Cut a slit in the end of the flap furthest away from the hindquarter and hook it over the leg. It will be held secure by the tendon. If you do the same with the other leg, you will now have a pack with the flaps of skin over your shoulder and the hindquarters on your back.

- I generally don't bother taking the forequarters out unless my animal is a larger Red or a Sika stag, because there is not a lot of meat on the shoulders. Best to bone out what you can.

NB Another alternative is to leave the hindquarters intact. To do this you will first need to gut the animal. Remove the back steaks as before but instead of cutting the legs off at the ball joint, cut the spine diagonally at a spot immediately in front of the hindquarters. Best to do this from the inside of the animal. Hey presto — you'll be smiling. Find the right spot and it's so easy you'll think you're a pro. Then follow the steps as outlined above to use the flaps of skin to make a pack.

TO BONE OUT THE LEGS AND REMOVE THE BACK STEAKS

If you want to take the undercut steaks you will first need to gut the deer, otherwise just follow the instructions. Your goal is to remove the bone, but leave the leg intact.

1] Remove the back steaks as above.

2] Cut the leg off at the ball joint, but don't cut the skin.

3] Carefully remove the leg from the skin, taking care not to get it dirty.

4] Once removed, lay it flat either on the skin or something clean with the inside of the leg facing up.

5] Follow the seams in the leg (i.e. where the muscles meet) and carefully pare the meat back from the bone. Once you have cut down to the bone it is easy then to run your knife along it and cut it away, leaving all the leg meat in one easy to handle pack.

Chapter 12   HOW TO CARRY OUT A DEER WHOLE

In the commercial hunting days, it was mandatory to carry out your deer whole if you wanted to sell it, but today most hunters either bone their meat out or carry out the hindquarters and back steaks, leaving the rest in the field. However, with increasing interest in small goods there is a good case now for taking out the whole animal, a skill that is largely lost on today's hunter.

FIRST GUT THE ANIMAL

If you have neck-shot or head-shot an animal, make sure you cut its throat as soon as possible to bleed the animal. Chances are the heart will still be beating, whereas if you shoot it through the chest it will bleed internally.

Steps to gutting an animal: our goal is to get all the insides of the deer out in one piece!

(NB This is how I do it. Others may do it differently.)

- Cut the deer's throat first. Then grab the deer's jaw and pull the head back to "break" the neck joint; then cut it off completely.

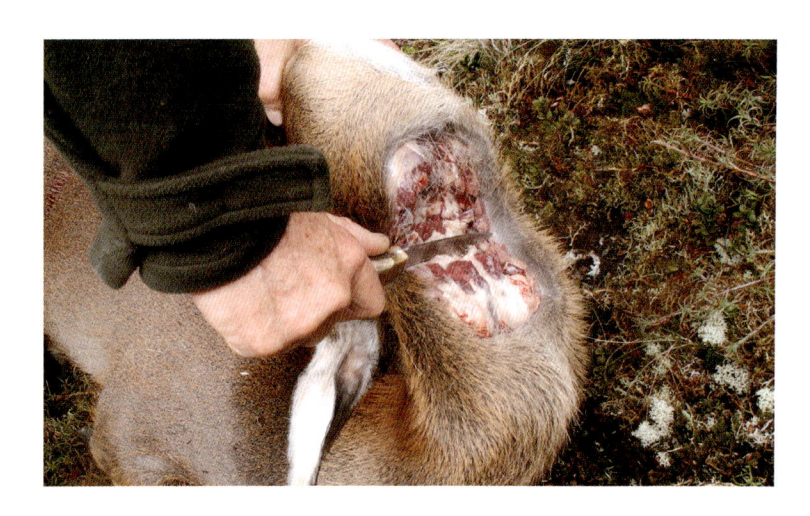

- Grab the voice box at the top of the wind pipe, pull it out and cut it off. That makes it easier to pull the wind pipe through.

- Make a slit at the base of the neck and reach in and pull the wind pipe down and out. Cut it off. DON'T cut up the deer's neck toward the head — leave the slit as small as possible.

- Now work on the bum end. At this stage, position the deer so that the hindquarters are facing uphill. If it is a stag, grab his penis and cut down each side of it. Hope you feel guilty as you do! You should be able to remove it almost from the animal. Leave the end nearest the backside attached. If it is a hind, cut off the udder. Now you need to cut around the ring gear i.e. the backside. Push your knife in and cut around in a circle — with a stag you can leave the penis attached at this point. Pull the backside out a bit so you can reach in further with your knife and cut around and make sure everything is free. Take care not to cut the bladder. If you do, you can bet it will be full, just as Murphy's law would say.

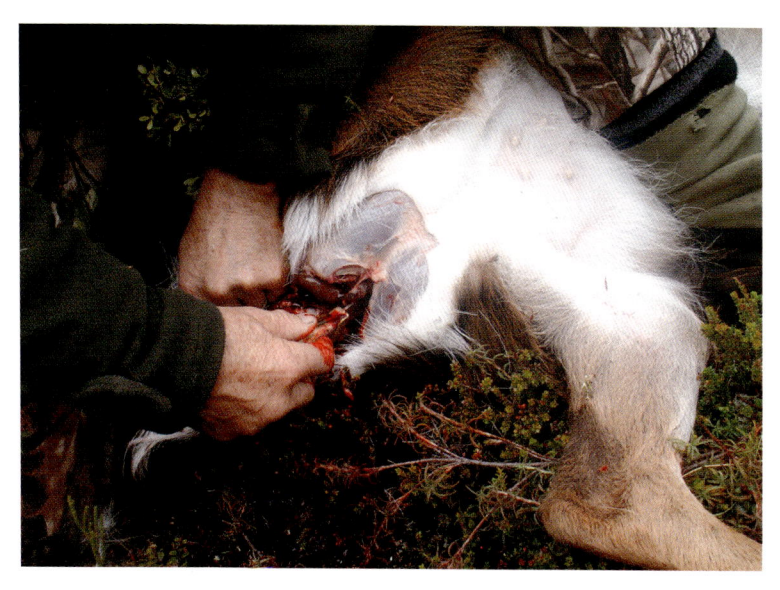

- Then make a slit in the deer's belly just in front of the hindquarters and, proceeding carefully, cut up the gut cavity to about the rib cage. Some hunters open the deer up from the brisket back. Please yourself. Try not to cut open the gut bag as the last thing you want is contamination from the stomach on the meat. This is where a drop point knife is very useful as you are less likely to dig the knife into the belly using this design. After first slitting open the belly, it's often helpful to run two fingers along each side of the knife, preventing the gut bag from being pierced.

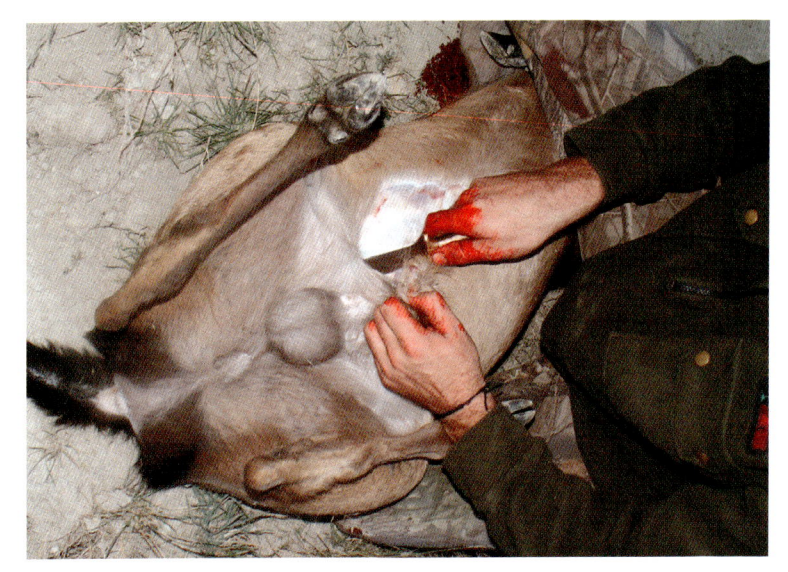

- Roll out the gut a little bit as best you can, so allowing you to reach in and make the next key cut. Take care NOT to break the gut bag open. DON'T pull it right away from the deer and DON'T cut it away from the diaphragm.

- Pull the deer around now so the head is partially uphill; reach in with your knife and cut the diaphragm around as far as you can. Take care not to cut the inside of the deer, as the less meat and gut that is cut the better. Remember that everywhere meat is cut, bacteria enters.

- At this point you should be able to reach in and grab the top of the heart and lungs and pull them out with the rest of the insides still attached. You may have to cut a bit more of the diaphragm and, as the rest of the guts follows, you may have to use your knife a little there also.

- Next you should be able to pull the ring gear out from the inside.

- Hey presto – with a little work you now have all the deer's insides on the ground, all together and nothing cut open to spill out over the meat to contaminate it. This presumes of course you have been clever and shot it in the neck or chest. What if you gut-shot it? We covered that briefly before. Wipe away as much of the spill-over from the gut as you can, using grass or a cloth if you have one.

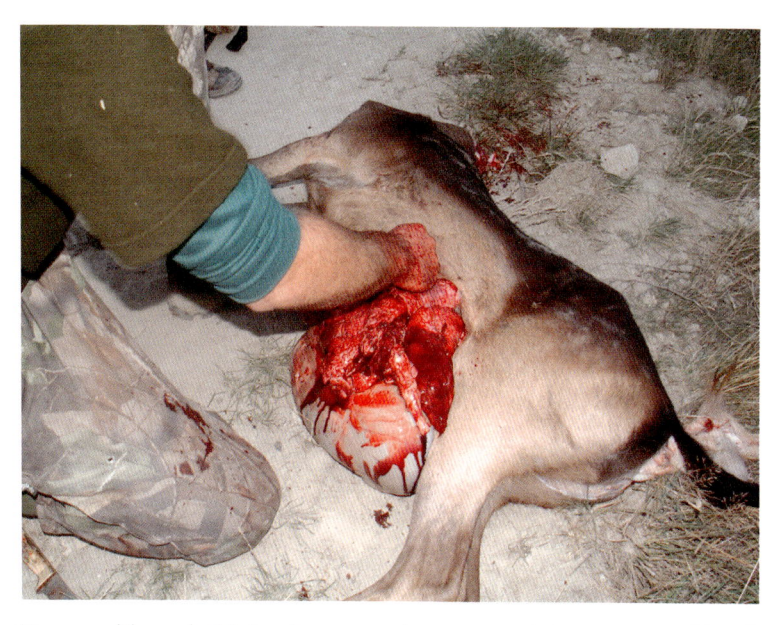

- You may like to hold the deer up at this stage and drain out any blood, especially if the animal has been chest-shot and bled internally. This is particularly important if the animal has been gut-shot as you need to get rid of as much of the spill-over from the gut bag as you can, as it is full of bacteria.

- If you are leaving the deer for any length of time, a good idea is to prop open the gut cavity with a stick and allow the air in to help cool the carcass down. Prop it up so it can drain if necessary. Yes, flies can be a real problem. When I was meat hunting in the days before the bureaucrats in Wellington and MAF got busy dreaming up ways to spoil our fun, I used to hang deer in trees for up to three days before they were collected and taken to a freezer. This was in summer too. I can't remember losing any either, although in those days enterprising meat buyers generally regarded a few maggots as extra weight!! But if meat is clean, and most of mine were neck shot, and it is kept cool and allowed to dry out inside, you'd be surprised at how long it will last, especially in winter.

There are various methods of carrying deer out whole:

1. USE A PACK FRAME

Probably the easiest method and one we used in the old meat hunting days primarily when hunting river flats. You simply strapped or tied one or two deer to the frame and off you went. However, the use of a pack frame in most cases today is not practical: in the bush they are simply a pain in the butt. Even while commercial meat hunting we seldom used them, and definitely not while bush hunting. The big advantage with a pack was when we carried out larger deer. They were definitely easier to handle with a pack frame.

2. PIKAU METHOD

Tying or hooking the front legs to the hind legs and carrying the deer upright on your back, with the neck directly behind and above your head or flopping to one side is the method depicted in many hunting stories and in some hunting videos. In my opinion this is a poor method of carrying out deer. There is a much better option, but more later!

This pikau-style method has a number of disadvantages:

a] The centre of gravity is quite high, making it easier for the hunter to lose his balance.

a] The neck flops around and has the potential to catch on branches, and it is difficult to duck under branches etc. simply because of the height of the animal sticking out above your head, especially when the animal stiffens up a bit.

b] It is a bit tough on your shoulders also and you can carry only one deer at a time, not that that seems to be an issue today.

c] If you shoot say two yearlings and want to carry both out, tough! You will have to make two trips.

Michael Edwards finds it a bit of a challenge carrying out a deer using this pikau method.

d] If you have a day bag which you carried on your shoulders, you now have nowhere to put it.

e] It's relatively awkward to carry your rifle, and your hands are definitely not free to shoot another deer!

f] Safety issues: The fact that you have a large amount of animal in view as you carry it out can be a safety issue, although one wonders why anyone could confuse a dead vertical deer on someone's back with the real McCoy. However, if you were to bend over, apart from the missing head, one would see a deer, and a trigger-happy excited hunter could be forgiven for thinking it was the real thing! (Hang a strip of orange around the neck and body if you are still determined to use this method!)

g] The only advantage of this method is that you need only a knife or a couple of bits of string to prepare the animal to carry out. I note that with pigs this method is often used because the majority of the weight of a big pig is in the shoulders.

3. USE A CARRY BELT

The third method is one I stumbled upon while hunting Fallow deer in the Blue Mountains many years ago. After getting rather frustrated by other methods, I got to thinking about the challenge one day and figured there had to be an easier and more efficient method. There is!

THE CARRY BELT METHOD

Using a carry belt is the author's preferred method of carrying out deer. Waldo Andersen is the model.

Note that you are in a good position to shoot another deer if you see one, or to use your hands to grab branches for support etc.

For this you will need to:

- Gut your animal as described above.

- Cut a slit about 8cm long above each of the knee joints. With the animal lying on its back and the legs up, your cut will be below the joint from your perspective. If you intend to keep the skin, you will need to cut down the inside of the leg carefully and then peel the skin back so as to avoid leaving holes in it.

Then remove the leg at the joint after you have cut a slit in it for the belt.

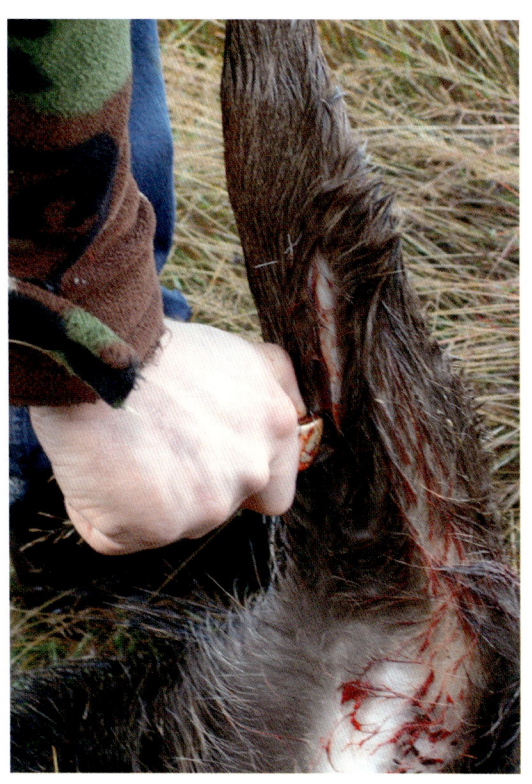

- Position the deer so that when you are facing it, the hindquarters are on your left. For a left-handed shooter you may have the hindquarters on the opposite side for reasons I will explain later. Now you will need a long belt; I use a leather belt 1.5 metres long, or you can use an old car seat belt.

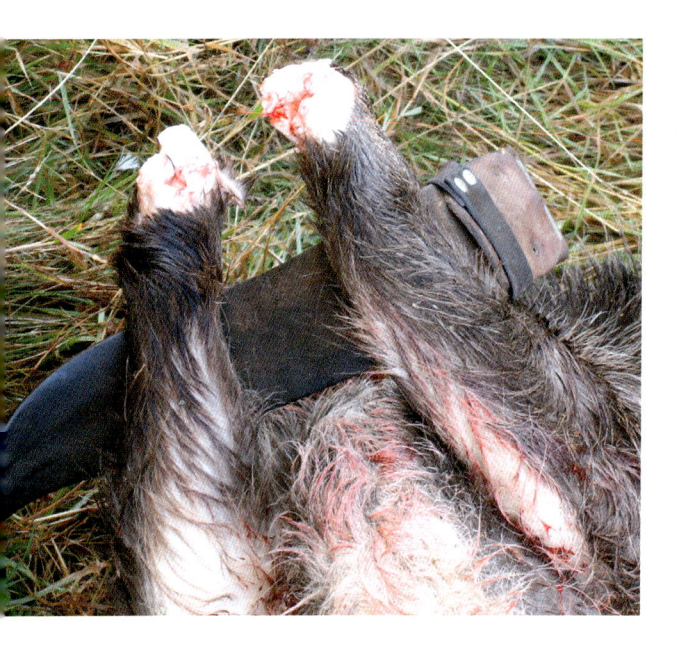

- Take your belt and, beginning with the front leg closest to you, thread your belt through the slits — two front legs first and then the hind legs. You can then link up the belt in the front, but don't tighten it up. Make sure the belt is pulled right through so the buckle is hard up against the front leg.

- Then with the animal propped up against a bank or suchlike with the four legs sticking up, sit down with your back to the deer and first place your left hand between the two front legs. Now place your right hand between the two hind legs. At this stage you will have the belt between the front and rear legs closest to you, behind your shoulders, so you can now reach over and pull it over your head. An alternative method is to leave the belt unconnected in the front and when you have your arms through the front and rear legs simply do up the belt. I prefer the first option.

- Tighten the belt and adjust its positioning on your shoulders.

- Now lean forward and stand up. If the animal is a heavy one, roll over on your knees before standing up. The deer can be released easily from your back simply by pulling on the belt flap and releasing the belt. I have used a rifle sling for this method, but it is easier on the shoulders with a slightly wider belt.

ADVANTAGES

- Your centre of gravity is quite low, making it easier to keep your balance.

- The animal is less visible, an important safety factor.

- If you have to duck under branches, no hassle! There is nothing sticking up to catch on branches etc.

- You can release the animal from your shoulders almost immediately by undoing the belt.

- You have both hands completely free. I've actually shot deer while carrying another out with this method and in fact while hunting Fallow, I used to carry on stalking with a deer on my back.

- You can also carry out more than one deer at a time by simply attaching the four legs of the second animal on the part of the belt between the front and rear legs across your back. I've carried three Fallow deer out

Frank Heaysman shows how it's done.

A bit of a challenge with this shot! Too bad if you wanted just the yearling – a neck shot wouldn't be a good idea, but a heart shot would scrape in. I'd be tempted to neck shoot the hind and then bowl the yearling. More to carry, but what fun!

- Individually hand-crafted
- Hand ground convex edge design
- Warranted for life against breakage under normal use
- Highest quality Swedish carbon tool steel
- Meticulously tempered blades
- We don't use stainless steel
- Made by B.W.Baker - Master Cutler
- New Zealand's finest – knives for a lifetime.

SVORD KNIVES
Smith Rd, RD2, Waiuku, Ph: **09 2358846**,
Fax: **09 2356483**, Email: **svord@xtra.co.nz**,
Web: **www.svord.com** *Free Catalogue available*

AT LAST! The ultimate weapon in testing rifles and ammunition

▶ **THE RETURN TO BATTERY MACHINE REST**
completely eliminates the possibility of human error when sighting in rifles or testing specific ammunition loads.

Call Custom Cartridges today to ensure your rifle is performing to its absolute best.
38 B Arthur Cres. P.O. Box 794 Taupo. Ph: 07 378 4593 Email: mark@nzsika.co.nz
www.customcartridges.co.nz

together like this.

- You can also bone out a second animal or take the hindquarters and back steaks and stuff them all inside the first animal — no way will they come out.

- If you have a day bag you can stuff it into the empty cavity of the deer or attach it to the belt where it runs across your back.

The reason I have the hindquarters on my right hand side is this — I like playing with the tail! No, just kidding: I carry my rifle in my right hand and when you have the neck hanging on that side it is a proper pain. For the record, I have carried out deer weighing about 100kg using this method — not much fun — but I regularly carried out stags of over 80kg and sometimes two hinds together. I've also carried out a number of pigs using this method, but, as stated previously, with a large pig the weight is very much in the front shoulders, so using this method could make you a little unbalanced.

I took out a bush patent on this method, but am still waiting for payments from hunters who use it!

A Good Tip – if you are transporting the full carcass of a deer any distance in a vehicle, especially if it is still a bit warm, purchase a bag of ice and place it in the chest cavity to cool it down. That should prevent any tainting of the meat.

A fired bullet is one thing you can't call back.

Chapter 13 IN CAMP

Keeping your meat safe in camp:

Many huts have meat safes, but some of these are suspect in that they are old and may not be fly-proof. A couple of years ago I had a short trip into the Hanamahihi clearings in the Urewera National Park in November, with my son Tim and one of his mates, Matt Rhodes. We were after big Rusa stags, but one day when the boys surprised a couple of Reds not too far from the hut, the temptation was too great. Now the hut had no safe, so we hung the meat in the shade in the trees, hoping to keep the flies at bay. However, the overcast and warm conditions meant that that was a tall order and after a couple of days, when the chopper was due, a quick inspection proved what I suspected — the only place the meat was going was in the river. No meat safe meant no meat.

Years ago when MAF got real fussy, and fly-blows were a guarantee your previously friendly meat buyer would break out in rashes and reject your animal, we made up some muslin bags, but these were pretty makeshift and often the flies still blew the meat through the bag, necessitating some deft knife work. Now Stoney Creek have made a portable meat safe that is large enough for several deer or a Wapiti should you collect one. It weighs 300g and comes in a very small pack, easy enough to carry without any hassle. It is easy to erect and the price is right. You could chuck one in your pack if you were away spring hunting or fly camping for a few days, and your meat would be safe. Make sure you hang it somewhere cool and out of the sun.

Stoney Creek meat safe weighs just on 300 grams and can easily hold a couple of deer. See www.stoneycreek.co.nz

If you haven't got a meat safe, hang your meat high up a tree, in the shade if possible and pray! A bit of pepper on the meat can also help keep flies at bay.

Chapter 14 — KEEPING YOUR SKINS

Grateful thanks to Trevor Chappell for this section. Trevor, who is based in Taupo and runs the 'Great Lake Tannery & Expediter', has had years of experience in preparing skins for hunters and trophy head skins for taxidermists

FOR FLAT SKINS

It is surprising the number of hunters who decide to get a deer skin tanned for a floor after the animal has been dragged down forest floors, across rivers, strung up in trees and maybe butchered on the ground. I guess you could say some are optimists. If you have taken a deer with a nice skin that you think would make an attractive addition to your trophy room or lounge floor you need to think carefully about two things:

1] The method of skinning

   While there are at least nine ways of skinning a cat, and most hunters have considered all of them, it's a little different when you come to skin a deer! For one, you don't have to worry about what the neighbour will think! Seriously though, think carefully about where the cuts on the underside of the animal will go. First prop the animal on its back so that cuts along the front and back legs are in the same place. The main cut down the stomach should start at the anus (backside) and finish at the neck. Try not to cut the hocks for carrying or stringing up to a branch, as these unnecessary cuts detract from the tanned skin. Carefully use a sharp knife to separate the hide from the carcass ie. around the legs and stomach. If the skin is being removed from around a warm carcass, then separation of the skin from the animal's body can be achieved by "punching" — that is by using the fist as a ball to forcefully separate the skin from the body. This, however, is extremely hard to do when the carcass is cold. In this case you will need to use your knife for the whole process.

2] Your care of the skin once you have removed it

   If a skin is warm, it is essential to cool it immediately once removed. You can easily achieve this by hanging it in a shady spot under a tree where a cool breeze can remove the heat. Realise that it is heat that generates the bacteria that will cause hair loss or slip. Better still, if you have plain (non-iodised) salt available, apply this to start the preserving process. Salt leaches the damaging body juices out of the skin while at the same time "fixing" the hair to prevent slip. While one salting is sufficient in the hills, a second thick coat of salt should be applied once you are home to ensure the skin stays preserved until the tanning process begins. Best to get it to your tanning professional ASAP.

3] Once tanned

You can enhance the life of your tanned skin by placing it where there is little foot traffic and by keeping it out of direct sunlight, as ultra violet light will cause it to become brittle and fade.

Author's note: If you intend to carry out the whole animal and keep the skin as well, you will have to compromise. Alternatively, you can bone it out in the field and take the skin — it just takes a little more care, as you want to keep the meat clean and at the same time keep the skin in good nick.

No regrets — that's how it should be.

Chapter 15   IF YOU SHOOT A TROPHY

Grateful thanks to Vern Pearson, from SIKA COUNTRY TAXIDERMY LIMITED for these pertinent comments. Vern is a fantastic taxidermist, and in 2004 he won the 'Judge's Choice' for the best taxidermy at the Sika Contest and Outdoor Game Show.

As a taxidermist I am always amazed at the number of hunters out there who are trying to shoot a trophy for the wall, yet don't know how to take the head skin off correctly for the modern shoulder mount. It is not difficult — take the time to learn before that magic day comes.

HEADSKINNING FOR SHOULDER MOUNTS

1] Opening cuts (as per diagram) — cut around the body behind the front legs, next cut around the front legs just above the knee, then up the back of the leg (not the inside) and out to the cut around the body. Another method is to simply sleeve-skin the legs with no cuts. From a point 5cm behind the base of the antlers/horns, cut down the top of the neck, following the dorsal line to the cut around the body. Next cut from the base of each antler/horn to the centre cut, forming a "Y".

2] Carefully skin off the shoulders and neck and remove head with the cape attached. It's generally easier to complete the head skinning back at camp or at home. Always allow the skin and head time to cool before packing.

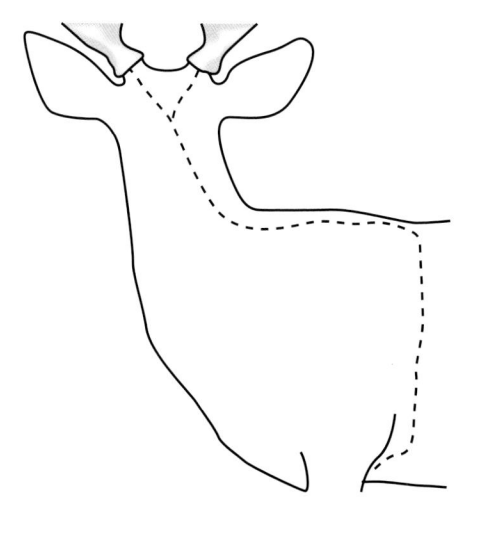

3] To remove the skin from the head, skin down the sides of the head, cutting off the ears close to the skull. Don't cut around the base of the antlers; instead cut up under the skin and pry off the skin around the coronet. A large screwdriver can be helpful here. With horned animals hold the hair down away from the horn and carefully cut around the base. Next is the eye: insert your index finger into the back corner of the eye and lift the skin, cutting at the same time as close as possible to the bone. Be careful not to cut through the skin at the front of the eye. All of our deer species have a gland in front of the eye (pre-orbital gland), which recesses into the skull. Carefully pry the skin out of the recess with the tip of your knife or a screwdriver. Next we come to the mouth: insert your finger into the corner of the mouth and pull the lip away while cutting close to the bone. Leave as much lip skin as possible. Cut through the nostril cartilage, leaving about 15mm of the nostril tubes on the skin.

4] The skin is off — if you are at home roll up skin to skin, seal in a plastic bag, label and freeze. If you are freezing the skin DON'T salt it. If you are remaining in the field for more than a couple of days you will have to split the lips and nostrils, turn the ears and salt the head skin.

5] Hold the lips between the thumb and forefinger and open up with your knife. This is done to enable the salt to penetrate to the hair roots. You will also have to split the nose cartilage down the middle between the nostril openings. Salt will only penetrate about 5mm of flesh, so anything thicker has to be thinned down. To turn the ears, cut between the ear cartilage and the skin at the back of the ear until the ear cartilage is clearly seen. Then with a spoon handle or steel etc., carefully push up between the skin and the cartilage to the tip and edges of the ear. Turn inside out and remove the flesh from the ear butt. Don't remove the ear cartilage.

6] Spread the skin out and liberally cover with PLAIN salt and rub in and out to the edges, ensuring it is completely covered. Roll up skin to skin and place in a muslin type bag to drain — DON'T PUT IN A PLASTIC BAG. Leave for 24 hours and resalt. The average head skin will require between 1 and 2kg of plain salt, depending on size.

7] REMEMBER IT IS BETTER TO HAVE TOO MUCH SKIN THAN NOT ENOUGH — WHAT WE DON'T HAVE WE CAN'T MOUNT.

8] HAPPY HUNTING!

1] To begin head skinning your trophy, cut a "Y" line from behind the ears to the back of each coronet.

2] Begin to peeel the skin off, taking care around the ears.

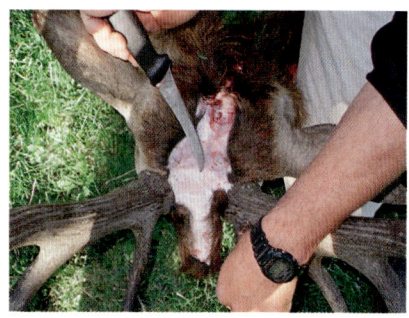

3] If you can, turn the ears, or leave for later.

4] Cut off the ear at the start of the cartilage.

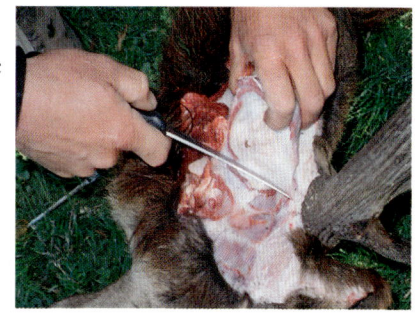

5] Take great care around the eye. It is easy to cut through the skin if you are not careful.

6] Cut inside the mouth to release the skin from the jaw.

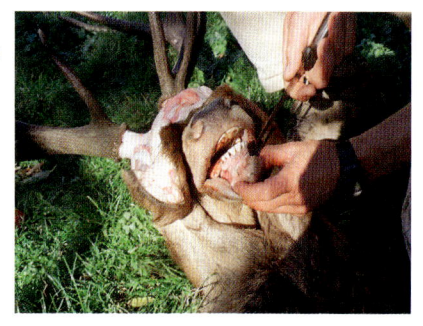

7] Peel the skin down towards the nose and cut off from behind nose cartilage.

PART THREE

PREPARING YOUR MEAT

- § Cutting it up yourself
- § What your butcher wants
- § A new worl of options
- § Storage.

I'd recommend that anyone who knows very little about butchery either talks to their butcher or goes on line and looks at the following web site: www.askthemeatman.com This is an American website that contains valuable information about butchering deer.

Identify your target ... at all times.

Chapter 16

CUTTING IT UP YOURSELF

Tenderising your meat by hanging it

It is generally a good idea to hang wild game for a few days in order to let enzymes work and tenderise it. Having said that, fresh back steaks, so fresh they are still kicking, are exceptionally tender and tasty, especially when you are tired and hungry after a day in the scrub.

The length of time you hang an animal depends on a number of factors: time of year, heat, humidity, air circulation, where it is shot and the age of the animal. A younger animal is generally more tender and requires less hanging time. An animal that has been gut-shot already has a good dose of bacteria at work.

Leave the skin on, as that means only one face or surface of the meat is exposed. If it's winter and you can keep it cool and protected from flies, you could hang it for several days or even a week or more. Down south where I originally came from, probably even much longer! In the summertime a day may be too long unless you have a chiller or similar. I generally hang mine in the garage, but I have to be careful to make sure no flies are around, and in summer it is less than ideal as it becomes quite warm with little ventilation. You can also help tenderise your meat by leaving it in the fridge for a few days after you have processed it.

To be truthful there are many and varied opinions as to how long you should hang meat for and how it should be left. One writer from Scotland said this: "Humidity and air circulation have the most dramatic effect. In chilly November (June in NZ), if it is teeming with rain, venison carcasses can reach ample maturity in six or seven days, but, if the weather is dry, those same carcasses will happily mature for three weeks or more", and "I believe that venison matures to a superior flavour when it is skinned first — the surface dries and the meat inside is sublime. When hung in the skin, it never sets so well and is more difficult, often impossible, to skin and butcher properly".

It is usually the Irish who are different, but, as you can see, maybe variety is the spice of life after all!

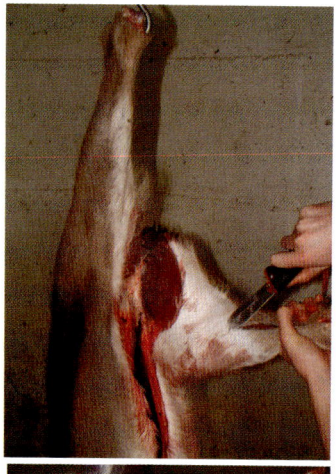

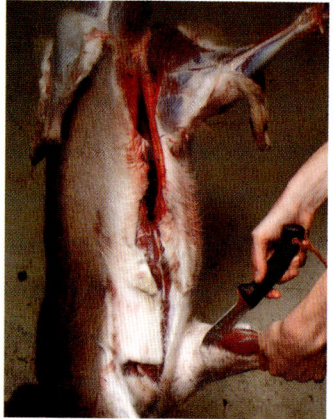

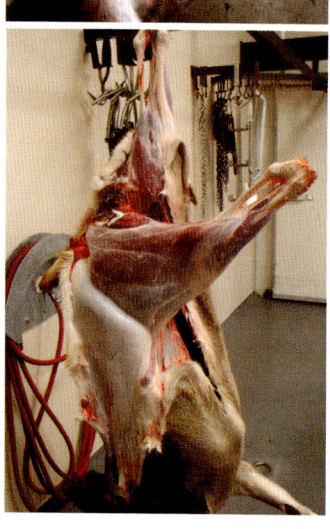

TO SKIN AN ANIMAL

The Americans tend to skin their animals from the neck to the tail, whereas we tend to do it in the reverse order. I've always skinned them bum to neck.

Here's how I do it:

1] Hang it up by its hindquarters, with its back legs spread.

2] Cut down the inside of both legs and begin to peel back the skin.

3] Cut around the "top" of the leg just below where you have attached it to a meat hook or similar.

4] You will need to cut the tail bone as you pull the skin down, and then continue removing the skin from the hindquarters and ribs.

5] Cut down the front legs in a similar fashion to what you did with the hind legs.

6] Cut down the front of the neck.

7] You should then be able to pull and cut the skin off.

HOW TO CUT UP A DEER

This part is in two sections (A) A written section for those who like to read about things and (B) A photographic 'how to' for those who are more visual!

A] Thanks to John Clarke for the tips on this section. John is a keen hunter and a butcher by trade. Read all these steps before you proceed, follow them and you will successfully bone out a deer. A suggestion here — talk to a local butcher, get together a few mates and put on an evening where he will show you how to cut up a deer, tell you where to look for disease indicators and show the right gear and how to sharpen knives. You will find it's well worth while — most of us learn better by seeing rather than just reading about it. Another good idea is to purchase a proper boning knife. You'll find it will make the task of boning out an animal much easier.

1] With the carcass hanging by the two back legs, mark down both sides of the back bone right to the neck, using a sharp knife.

2] Now move so the gut cavity of the carcass is facing you. Cut the Achilles tendon on the left leg. At this stage let the leg drop over. With a sharp saw cut the bone joining the pelvic cavity (the aitch bone). It will be facing you.

3] Using your knife, cut down until you reach a cup-type joint.

4] Next, carefully cut down close to the exposed bone, ensuring not to slash any of the meat. This is your rump steak. Once clear, the left leg should hang limp, enabling you to concentrate on the next procedure. NB: Do not cut the leg off.

5] Move again so that the back of the carcass is facing you. Care must be taken not to rush the next part so as to avoid damaging the back steaks or the porterhouse. Using the tip of your knife cut the back steaks clear from the bone until you reach the ribs, then in even strokes cut the meat away from the ribs until you are able to remove the entire side from the rest of the carcass. The hindquarter, back steak, rib cage meat and front shoulder should all come away in one piece.

6] Repeat on the other side, except that here the rib cage will fall away from the meat, leaving the side hanging from the hook.

7] Cut the sides into three pieces — leg, loin and shoulder. The loin can be cut, leaving a short tail at the end of the back steaks. The rest of the meat from the loins can go into making small goods, as can any other scrap meat.

8] Make a cut below the exposed ball joint, removing the piece of meat — this is the rump. Now turn the leg so that the tendon is away from you. A visible line on the left outside of the leg will reveal a seam. Clear this with a sharp knife, cutting upwards to the knee cap or the patella. Next make an incision from the ball joint up the leg on the inside of the leg, hard against the bone or femur up to the knee cap, carefully removing the thick flank. Next lay the leg on its back or outside. Make an incision from the knee cap, cutting in a direction to the right until you reach another diagonal seam. Once you reach the seam follow it downwards, carefully removing the topside. Now turn the leg over and cut away the rest of the meat, removing both the silverside and shin meat. Lay the silverside on its back or outside and remove the shin from the tail end of the silverside. That's it for the leg!

9] The Forequarter: Most hunters usually shoot their deer in this area and as a result the meat is often damaged beyond use. However, usually some meat can be salvaged. Cut away the best pieces and use them to make small goods.

B] Thanks to Andrew Elmiger for this visual record. Andrew is also a keen hunter and a butcher by trade. Descriptions here to go with the relevant photos. (Note: Andrew is using a proper boning knife.)

1] This is your goal — to remove a side of the animal in one piece.

2] With your deer hanging up by a hind leg, begin to cut down the side of the back bone.

3] Cut down on both sides of the backbone.

1

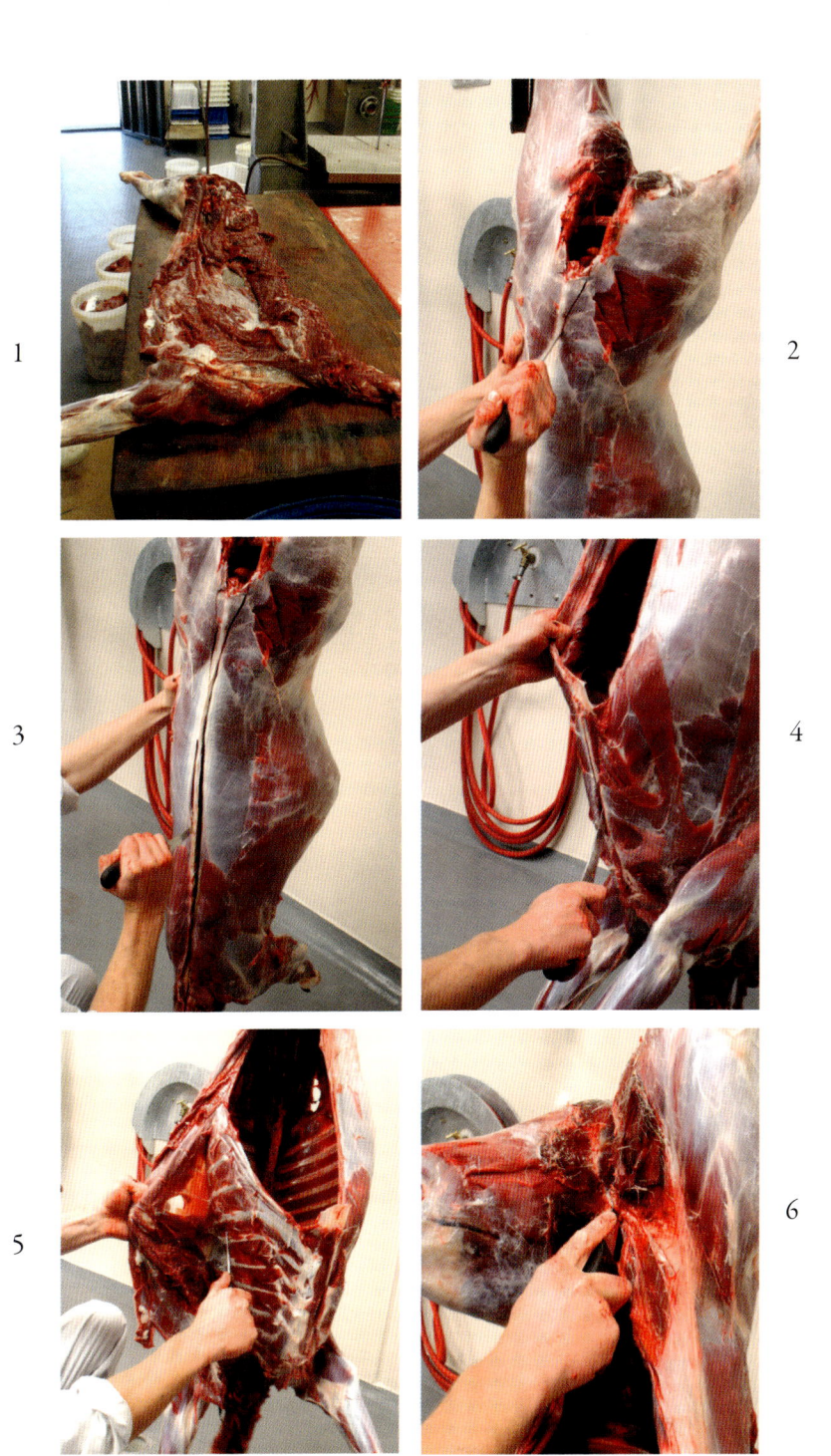

2

3

4

5

6

111

4] Cut down the brisket.

5] Begin to take off the side of the deer, starting with the neck. Note how much good meat you are removing from the ribs.

6 & 7] Then begin at the top of the hindquarter, cut down and expose the ball joint and continue to cut away the leg. When you have finished this, cut down the side of the undercut steaks (found at the rear of the backbone immediately in front of the hindquarters) and remove them.

8] Continue down keeping the knife close to the bone.

9] Here Andrew our butcher has cut a slit in the skirt and as he holds the leg up he continues cutting the back steak off the back bone until it all comes off in one piece and leaves only bone remaining.

10] After placing the side on a suitable surface, removal of the back steak is the next step. Front is normally sirloin, the rear portion rib eye.

11] The undercut steak may be small, but it is very tasty.

12] Here we have both back steak and undercut steak removed.

An innovative idea re the processing of back steaks is to slice the whole back steak in half along its length. You can then cut it up into generous sized portions ideal for the barbecue.

13] With the inside of the hindquarter face up, cut so as to remove the bone.

7

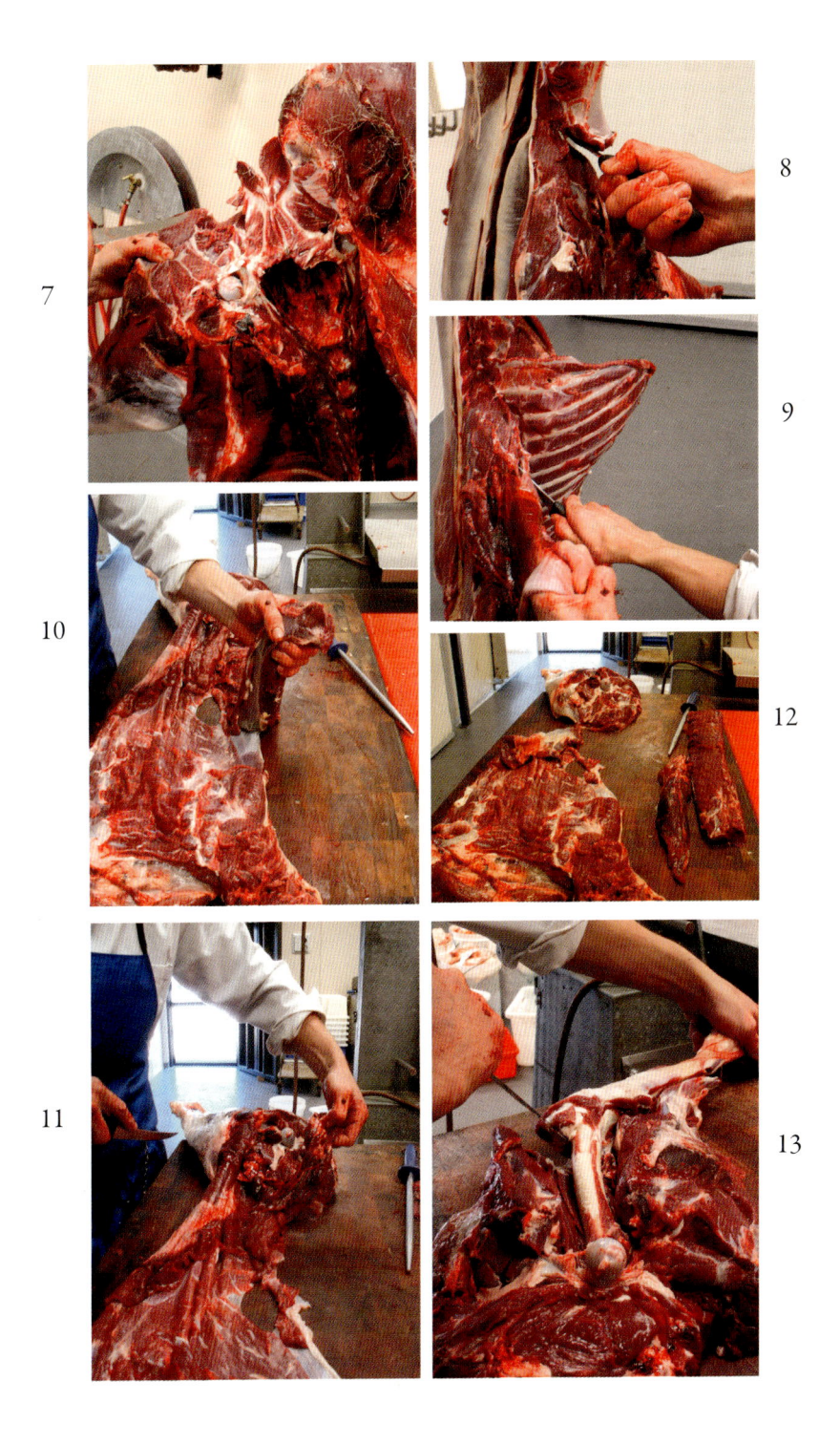

8

9

10

11

12

13

113

14] Once the bone is removed, you can separate the rump steak.

15] Now the meat is divided into muscle groups which can be used as steak, for casserole or roasting. With smaller deer you can leave two or more muscle groups together and cut them up for steak.

16] This photo shows a hindquarter of a deer and the skirt ready for packing or processing. Place the meat for small goods in something like a bucket or strong plastic bag to be taken to your butcher for processing.

17 & 18] Front shoulder is next — with the inside of the shoulder facing up, cut back the meat, exposing the joint, which you can cut through.

19] Remove the meat from the side of the shoulder facing up.

20] Next cut down both sides of the shoulder blade.

21] Turn it over and cut alongside both sides of the centre bone.

22 & 23] Turn it over again, remove the bone and cut away the meat. Meat from the front shoulder is best used for sausages or other small goods.

Repeat with the other side, the only difference being that you cut the frame of the carcass away from the side which is then left hanging ready for further processing.

You have done it — now you can enjoy eating it, knowing you have done a great job on the butchery!

14

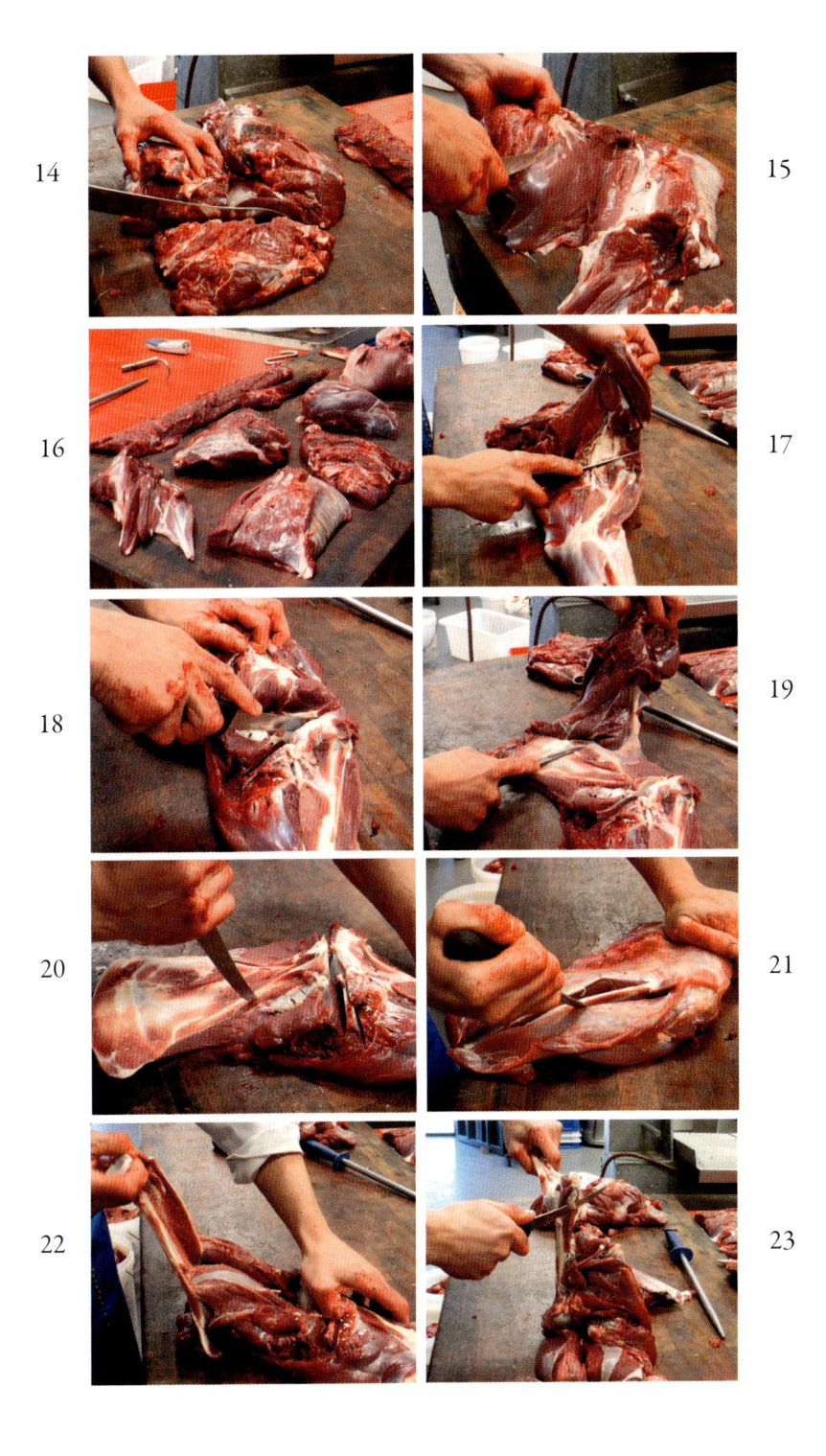

15

16

17

18

19

20

21

22

23

115

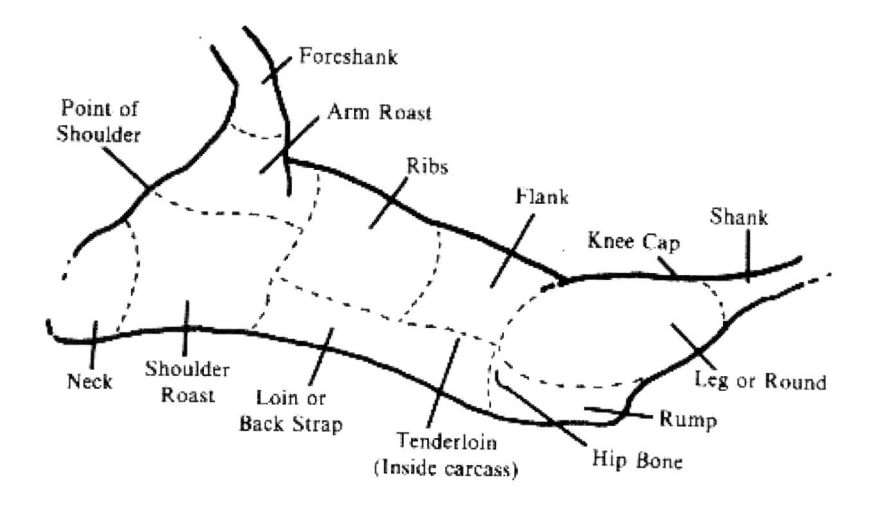

A diagram showing alternative cuts

Think at all times and be prepared.

Chapter 17   WHAT YOUR BUTCHER WANTS

You can have your butcher process the whole animal, or cut it up yourself, and then just ask him to process certain parts or the trimmings. For example you may give him a hindquarter, the front shoulders and trimmings and ask him to make them into sausages, jerky or salami. Whatever you give him he has one requirement: he wants <u>good, clean meat</u>.

He doesn't want meat covered with dirt, hair and fly blows! He hasn't time to clean your mess up and you will end up with a poor product! If you bring in junk, that is what you will get back.

Keep your trimmings in a 10 litre plastic container in your freezer until it is full and then he can convert these into a number of different quality products.

If you have carried out a whole deer, you may have butchered it at home and have left the shoulders and the neck, wondering what to do with them. You can bone out the shoulders as trimmings and keep the neck to be cut up by your butcher with a band saw for casserole meat. Neck meat is very tender, but is quite difficult to bone out.

Talk to your butcher or one of the butchers mentioned in this book — they all specialise in processing venison products.

Please note that if you want a butcher to process your meat they need to be registered as a home kill provider and recreational catch service provider. You can check on this by going to the following web site: www.nzfa.govt.nz/animalproducts/subject/homekill/index.htm

Also if hunters are selling the meat, it needs to come through the regulated system, i.e. the hunter needs to be a certified supplier and the meat needs to be processed in premises registered by NZFSA.

You can check on this by going to the following web site.

www.nzfsa.govt.co.nz/animalproducts/subject/hunting-wild-animals

Chapter 18   A NEW WORLD OF OPTIONS

All game meats can be processed in some form of useable small goods, continental or smoked meat. Blends of meat such as venison and pork and venison and mutton can be great. Here are some examples of what you can make out of your venison, particularly your trimmings and offcuts.

- Pastrami — meat that is cured, coated with a variety of peppers and then smoked.

- Ham.

- Bacon.

- Salamis — probably the most popular venison byproduct. A huge variety of flavours available. Just ask.

- Biersticks — a mini salami. Again there are hundreds of recipes. These are great to take into the hills and to eat as a snack while hunting.

- Continental smoked sausage.

- Burger patties — great for easy cooking in camp.

- Meat loaves.

- Sausages — all your offcuts and trimmings can be made into sausages or sausage meat. Even better mixed with mutton or pork fat.

- Sausage meat.

- Luncheon.

- Jerky — dried meat.

- Biltong — African-style jerky. The meat is cut into thick slices, flavoured with spices and air dried. Very tasty. You can turn all your good cuts into biltong.

- Dried sausage.

- Corned venison.

Give hunting a clean image — take your rubbish home.

Chapter 19 · STORAGE

After you have cut your meat up, chill it for a few days in the fridge at, say, between 2 and 4 degrees, prior to freezing. This helps the meat fibres to break down. The meat fibres will not break down if the meat is frozen immediately. Mark your bags and remove as much air from them as possible before freezing.

Be prepared — take the right gear.

PART FOUR

ENJOY! RECIPES and TIPS

- § Venison Recipes, compliments of Deer Industry New Zealand
- § Venison Recipes — General
- § Homemade jerky
- § Recommended books

Got your map and compass?

Chapter 20 — VENISON RECIPES, COMPLIMENTS OF DEER INDUSTRY NEW ZEALAND

The author would like to express his grateful thanks to Deer Industry New Zealand for permission to use the following information and selected venison recipes. Check out their web site www.nzvenison.com for further information and a complete list of amazing mouth-watering recipes! All you need to complement these is a nice glass or two of quality New Zealand red wine.

Simple and versatile

Being so lean and naturally tender, New Zealand Venison takes little effort to prepare. It's best cooked quickly, over a high heat and served lightly and simply to make the most of its unique taste — quick, simple, and simply delicious — perfect for busy, modern lifestyles.

An incredibly versatile product, New Zealand Venison is perfect for any style of cuisine — its use is limited only by your imagination. Try it in a salad, in a stir-fry, atop a pizza, as a spicy satay or in your favourite pasta dish. It's also ideal for the barbecue as a steak, medallions, or kebabs. Its versatility, ease of use and year-round availability make New Zealand Venison an ideal choice for any season.

Cooking Tips

- Always pre-heat the oven, grill, heavy fry pan or barbecue before cooking New Zealand Venison.

- There is no need to marinate New Zealand Venison, which is naturally tender if cooked correctly. However, sauces or brief marinades may be used as an accompaniment or light flavour enhancement.

- The most critical factor is not to overcook New Zealand Venison. Because it is so lean, overcooking may cause dryness. Cook New Zealand Venison quickly over high heat and serve rare or medium rare for maximum flavour and tenderness.

- Rest venison after cooking, either covered, or in a warm place, for 5–10 minutes, depending on the size of the cut, before serving. This will allow natural juices to disperse evenly. Do not reheat New Zealand Venison unless it is in a casserole.

- Like other meat, New Zealand Venison should not be eaten raw or undercooked during pregnancy or by people with weakened immune systems.

Peppered Roast

HERBED VENISON WITH BALSAMIC TOMATOES

Chef Ruth Pretty

INGREDIENTS

1 tbsp finely grated lemon rind
1 garlic clove (crushed)
2 tbsp finely chopped parsley
½tsp freshly ground black pepper
1 rack of venison (approx 1.2kg and trimmed of silverskin)
520g (6) tomatoes
Sea salt and freshly ground black pepper
30mls (2 tbsp) extra virgin olive oil
30mls (2 tbsp) balsamic vinegar
70g–140g (4–8 tbsp) Sun-dried Tomato Pesto
4–8 handfuls salad greens
extra virgin olive oil

METHOD

Preheat oven to 220°C.

Combine lemon rind, garlic, parsley and pepper. Rub onto outside of venison rack.

Cut tomatoes crosswise into 3 thick slices and arrange in a lightly oiled non-reactive roasting tray. Sprinkle tomatoes with salt, pepper, oil and balsamic vinegar.

Place venison rack on tomatoes and roast for 20–25 minutes, or until the venison is cooked medium rare. Test by pressing your thumb into the meat. If the meat feels loose then it is rare; if it offers you some resistance then it is cooked medium rare; if it is firm you have overcooked it.

Remove from oven and cover tray with heavy tea towels or a towel and away from heat allow the venison to rest for at least 10 minutes. This will distribute the meat juices.

Slice the venison into single cutlets.

Arrange tomatoes on 4 (or 8) warmed dinner plates and arrange venison cutlet(s) on top of tomatoes. Accompany with a dollop of sun-dried Tomato Pesto. Place some salad greens next to the venison and drizzle plate with extra virgin olive oil.

Like other meat, New Zealand venison should not be eaten raw or undercooked during pregnancy or by people with weakened immune systems.

VENISON RAGOUT WITH BERRIES

INGREDIENTS

500g venison (diced in 1cm cubes)
1tsp paprika
½tsp dried thyme or 1tsp fresh thyme
Salt and black pepper
100ml vegetable oil
½ cup finely diced carrot, leek and celery
2 cloves crushed garlic
1 rasher of bacon (finely sliced)
1 clove garlic
100ml red wine
½tsp vinegar (red wine or balsamic)
1tbsp tomato paste
1tsp Dijon mustard
Zest of ½ lemon
70g cranberries
100ml meat stock
1tbsp cornflour (mixed in water)
100ml crème fraîche

METHOD

Spice the venison with paprika, thyme and pepper. Fry it in a hot oil until well coloured and season with salt.

Add the diced vegetables, the garlic clove and the bacon and sauté until the vegetables are soft. Add the red wine. Then mix the vinegar, tomato paste, mustard and the lemon zests in and add the cranberries. Combine with the meat stock and let it simmer for about an hour. When the venison is tender, add the cornflour, heat it up gently and season with salt and pepper. Top the ragout with crème fraîche.

Like other meat, New Zealand venison should not be eaten raw or undercooked during pregnancy or by people with weakened immune systems.

VENISON ROULADE WITH ROAST GARLIC and HERB BUTTER

INGREDIENTS

4 venison leg fillets (180g per person)
8 slices of Parma ham
150g of unsalted butter
2 anchovies
4 cloves of roasted garlic
½ tsp of chopped rosemary, basil, thyme, parsley
1 tspn of coarse ground pepper

Sauce

3 chopped shallots or onion
½ cup of red wine
1 tsp balsamic vinegar
25g of butter or olive oil
½ cup of strong meat stock
Salt and pepper

METHOD

Use a sharp knife to cut the fillet along the grain about 6mm thick and roll out as you go to form a flat piece. Season with pepper. Lay the Parma ham out on a piece of non stick paper and place the venison on top. Mix the herbs and garlic with the softened butter and smear over the meat. Roll up tight and allow to set in the fridge.

Sear the meat all over for 2 minutes and finish in a moderate oven (180 degrees) for about 8 minutes; allow to rest in a warm place. In the same pan add the butter and the shallots and sauté until soft. Add the red wine and reduce to a syrup, add the meat stock and the balsamic vinegar to taste. Reduce a little and season.

Slice the meat into 3 pieces per fillet and place on a bed of the sautéed vegetables and garnish with some cherry tomatoes and the sauce.

Garnish

Medley of spring vegetables sautéed with a little butter and new potatoes roasted with sprigs of rosemary and garlic.

Like other meat, New Zealand venison should not be eaten raw or undercooked during pregnancy or by people with weakened immune systems.

CHARGRILLED NEW ZEALAND VENISON STEAKS WITH SUMMER VEGETABLES

INGREDIENTS

4 New Zealand venison steaks or medallions (allow approximately 4oz (125g) per serving)
A selection of seasonal vegetables of your choice —

> aubergines (or small courgettes)
> peppers (or scallopini)
> cocktail tomatoes
> mushrooms
> spring onions

1–2tbsp olive oil
½ tsp freshly ground black pepper
1 clove garlic, crushed (optional)
1–2tbsp marjoram, oreganum, rosemary, basil or chives finely chopped
Juice 1–2 lemons

NO MATTER WHAT...

You're new to hunting?
You've been hunting for years?
You're getting back into hunting?

YOU NEED TO JOIN HUNTERS & HABITATS CLUB

**If you care about going hunting tomorrow and beyond
JOIN TODAY**

FIND OUT MORE AND JOIN ONLINE
www.nzsika.co.nz

H&H HUNTERS & HABITATS

CONTACT MARK
Ph: (07) 378 4593, P.O. Box 794 Taupo NZ

HELIHUNT 'N' FISH TAUPO LTD

in association with Te Onepu Helicopters

Hunting, Tramping & Fishing Charters:

- Kaweka
- Kaimanawa
- Whirinaki
- Te Urewera
- Pureoras

Agricultural & Commercial:

- Spraying (dgps guided)
- Fertilizer
- Seeding
- Lifting
- Fire Lighting
- Fire Fighting
- Frost Protection

For more info contact Phil Janssen:
A/Hours: 07 3785314
Mobile: 0274 479350
Hanger: 07 384 2000
Email: p.janssen@xtra.co.nz

Based at Rangataiki (Napier- Taupo Road)

Noise Control

MAE is the only suppressor manufacturer in the southern hemisphere to offer the consumer, suppressors that are crafted from the highest quality materials. MAE can manufacture suppressors from exotic steels like titanium through to stainless. In UK tests, MAE's suppressors have been rated the quietest in it's class (Shooting Sports - May 2002 issue) formely PES. Thats something to make some noise about...

For more info:
website. www.mae.co.nz email. info@mae.co.nz phone. +64 9 443 2536

MAE SUPPRESSORS

METHOD

Brush steaks lightly with oil and dust with black pepper; leave for 30 minutes at room temperature. Prepare vegetables. Slice aubergines, or cut courgettes in half lengthways, halve peppers, remove core and seeds, halve tomatoes, trim stalks from mushrooms. Toss vegetables in oil, garlic and black pepper. Preheat grill or heavy-based fry pan. Grill or panfry New Zealand venison steaks over a high heat approximately 1½–2 minutes each side. Remove from heat while still rare and let rest about 4 minutes, covered with foil. Grill vegetables, adding spring onions, tomatoes and mushrooms last. Pour lemon juice over vegetables, sprinkle with chopped herbs and serve with New Zealand venison steaks.

To Barbecue — Heat grill plate thoroughly, brush with oil to prevent steaks sticking. Cook New Zealand venison steaks quickly, move to side of barbecue away from heat to complete cooking process. Brush vegetables with marinade while cooking. Cocktail tomatoes can be substituted with peeled half tomatoes.

Like other meat, New Zealand venison should not be eaten raw or undercooked during pregnancy or by people with weakened immune systems.

BRAISED TOPSIDE OF NEW ZEALAND VENISON

INGREDIENTS

1 cup red wine vinegar
1 cup water
5 whole allspice berries
8 peppercorns
1 tsp brown sugar
1 onion
1 bay leaf
1 carrot
1 stalk celery
1 sprig thyme

1½–2lbs (750g–1kg) topside New Zealand venison
8 juniper berries
6 black peppercorns
½tsp chopped thyme
1 onion
3 rashers bacon
1oz (25g) butter
½ cup red wine
12 prunes
1 peeled and diced apple
¼ cup walnut halves

METHOD

In a large saucepan place vinegar, water, whole allspice, peppercorns, brown sugar, sliced onion, bay leaf, sliced carrot and celery and sprig of thyme. Bring slowly to the boil and simmer for 30 minutes. Remove from the heat and allow to cool. Place the New Zealand venison piece in a non-metallic bowl, and pour over the cool marinade. Cover, and place in refrigerator for a minimum of 24 hours. Drain, reserving half a cup of marinade. Dry the meat with a paper towel. Tie the meat with string. Crush the juniper berries, black peppercorns and thyme together. Rub the surface of meat with the crushed mixture. Slice onion finely. Remove rind and chop the bacon. In a heavy-based casserole, heat the butter. Cook bacon and onions together until golden. Remove from casserole. Lightly brown meat in the residual butter. Return onions and bacon to casserole. Pour in reserved marinade and the wine, prunes, diced apple and walnuts. Cover tightly and simmer for 1½ to 2 hours until meat is tender. Serve with sauce spooned over.

Like other meat, New Zealand venison should not be eaten raw or undercooked during pregnancy or by people with weakened immune systems.

GRILLED NEW ZEALAND VENISON STEAK WITH ROSEMARY SCENTED INFUSION

INGREDIENTS

4tbsp balsamic vinegar

2tsp lime juice
4 garlic cloves, crushed
2tbsp fresh rosemary, chopped
½tsp freshly ground black pepper
pinch of chilli powder (optional)
2tbsp extra virgin olive oil
4 New Zealand Venison steaks

METHOD

To make the infusion — mix the first six ingredients together and slowly whisk in the olive oil. Place the New Zealand Venison steaks in a shallow dish. Spoon the infusion over the steaks, making sure they are well coated. Cover and refrigerate for 30 minutes. Cook the steaks on a barbecue or under a hot grill for 3–4 minutes on each side, basting frequently. Serve with barbecued or grilled polenta and a rocket salad lightly seasoned with lemon juice and olive oil.

Like other meat, New Zealand Venison should not be eaten raw or undercooked during pregnancy or by people with weakened immune systems.

ROAST SADDLE OF NEW ZEALAND VENISON

INGREDIENTS

1 saddle of New Zealand Venison (9½oz (300g) per person)
2 slices bacon, cut into strips
Salt
Freshly ground black pepper
3oz (60g) lard
1 parsley root, chopped
2 carrots, chopped
2 stalks celery, chopped
1 onion, chopped
8 fluid oz (1 cup) dry red wine
1 cup beef stock
6 juniper berries, crushed
2 bay leaves

6 peppercorns
2 sprigs thyme, chopped
8 fluid oz (1 cup) cream
Stewed peaches, halved, filled with cranberries

METHOD

Preheat the oven to 375°F (190°C). Skin the saddle and lard it with the bacon. Brown the saddle on all sides in the lard and season with salt and pepper. Remove the saddle from the frying pan. Lightly sauté the parsley, carrots, celery and onions without allowing them to brown. Add the wine, stock, juniper berries, bay leaves, peppercorns and thyme. Transfer to a roasting dish, place the saddle on top and roast in the preheated oven for 45 minutes. Make sure that the meat is still pink inside otherwise it will be dry and tasteless. Remove the meat from the roasting pan and keep it warm. Pass the cooking liquid through a sieve, pressing hard with a wooden spoon to extract all juices from the ingredients. Add the cream and season. To serve, cut the meat off the bone and slice. Serve the meat masked with the sauce, together with the peaches.

Like other meat, New Zealand Venison should not be eaten raw or undercooked during pregnancy or by people with weakened immune systems.

NEW ZEALAND VENISON BARBECUE SAUCE

INGREDIENTS

1 tbsp oil
2 medium onions, peeled, medium dice
3 branches celery, washed, medium dice
½ cup brown sugar
2 tbsp champagne vinegar
1½ cups orange juice
1½ tbsp chopped garlic
3 medium tomatoes, cored and diced large
26oz (800g) chopped tomatoes
14oz (400g) ketchup

2 tsp celery seeds
2 tbsp Worcestershire sauce
½tsp ground coriander
1 scant tablespoon ground cumin
2 tbsp salt
1½tsp red pepper flakes

METHOD

In a medium saucepan at medium-high heat, sauté onions and celery in oil. Meanwhile, in a smaller pot, combine sugar and vinegar and cook at high heat for approximately three minutes. Add orange juice to sugar mixture, cook one minute and reserve on the side. Add garlic to first pot and cook for two minutes. Add sugar mixture to first pot and bring to a simmer. Add remaining ingredients and simmer gently for 20 minutes. Blend sauce for four minutes at high speed until smooth.

Grilling

Rub New Zealand Venison with barbecue sauce approximately one hour before grilling. Grill at high heat approximately 10in (25.5cm) from heat source. Do not turn too frequently so as to allow the sauce to caramelise on the New Zealand Venison. Cook to a desired doneness; rare to medium-rare is optimum. Allow meat to rest approximately two to three minutes before slicing into ¼in (5mm) slices and serve. Optional suggestions — Served with sautéed then smoked onions. Serve with a small amount of red pepper aioli.

Like other meat, New Zealand Venison should not be eaten raw or undercooked during pregnancy or by people with weakened immune systems.

Chapter 21 — VENISON RECIPES – GENERAL

VENISON MARINADE

If you so desire, you can marinade venison — I sometimes use this marinade when preparing thin slices of back steaks for a barbecue:

INGREDIENTS

1 cup red wine
1 bay leaf
1 sprig thyme
2 cloves of garlic, crushed
1 onion chopped
Tsp brown sugar
Dash of soy sauce
Olive oil
Salt and ground pepper

METHOD

After mixing the marinade, pour over the meat and leave for 3 to 6 hours. Use enough olive oil so the meat is covered. Cook the meat for a few minutes on each side in hot pan with a little oil. Tastes real nice!

VENISON STEW

Variations of this recipe have been used since the year dot in New Zealand. You can simplify if in the bush!

INGREDIENTS

500gm venison
Flour
2tbsp oil
2 onions chopped
A clove of garlic — two, if you want to keep others at bay

1 cup red wine
2 carrots diced
500 grams tomatoes cut into small pieces, or a can of tomato puree
1tsp brown sugar
1tsp thyme
1tsp sage
Water
125g mushrooms cooked in butter
Seasoning

METHOD

Cut the meat into cubes, coat with flour and brown in oil with the onions. Place in a casserole dish or camp oven and cook for about 2½ hours at 160°C. If in a camp oven, cook slowly. Half an hour before serving add mushrooms and then thicken.

ROAST VENISON — OLD SCOTTISH RECIPE

This is an old Scottish recipe that I became acquainted with as a result of a friend's birthday party! As they had asked me for a leg of venison, I had a vested interest in the outcome. It was cooked by a chef for the occasion, and would be, without exception, the nicest venison I have ever tasted. It is different! Best cooked slightly rare.

INGREDIENTS

One leg of venison, about 3kg
A tablespoon of olive oil
Salt and black pepper
2tsp butter
200gm diced pork or bacon
<u>Marinade</u>
1 bottle of burgundy or claret
2 cloves garlic
1 bay leaf
2 carrots

1 large onion
1 tsp black peppercorns
1 sprig rosemary
2 crushed juniper berries
4tbsp olive oil

SAUCE

½ cup port wine
1 tbsp red currant or rowanberry jelly
Gravy from the venison
1tbsp flour
1tbsp butter

METHOD

For the marinade, slice and peel the onion and carrots, then cook them gently in olive oil, but do not let them brown. Put them into a glass or earthenware dish (not metal), add the wine, and other ingredients. Soak the venison in this, for about two days, turning several times a day, so that all the surfaces are coated with marinade.

When it is ready, take it out and dry it with a clean cloth. Combine the butter and oil in a heavy pan that has a tight lid, and when hot add the diced pork or bacon. Fry until the cubes are crisp, then add the joint, and brown on all sides. Reduce the marinade to half by boiling it rapidly on the top of the stove, and strain it over the venison. Season to taste and cook in the oven at 170°C for 30mins per 450 grams.

To make the sauce, strain off the pan juices, and reduce them again to half on top of the stove by boiling rapidly. Rub the flour into the butter, and add this to thicken it. Stir well, then add port and redcurrant, or rowan jelly, mixing it very well. Serve over venison or separately as desired.

Chapter 22

BEEF or VENISON JERKY
(Homemade)

This is great to throw in your day pack, as it can be chewed as a snack. It is light and high in protein. Jerky can be made from a variety of cuts — with beef the cheaper ones are adequate. Partially freezing the meat will make it easier to slice evenly. Cut across the grain if you want your meat tender!

You'll need the following:

Venison: approximately 1kg. Slice the meat into 1cm wide strips and make sure that all the fat and gristle is removed.

Mixture

¼ cup of soy sauce
1 tablespoon of Worcestershire sauce
¼ teaspoon each of pepper and garlic powder (flavour to suit yourself)
½ teaspoon of onion powder
1 tablespoon of hickory smoked salt

Make sure all the ingredients are dissolved when you make up the mixture. Then marinate the meat overnight in the mixture.

Next drain the meat and place strips on a grill rack or cake rack with the oven tray underneath to catch the drips. Bake the meat on a low heat (70°C) for about 10 hours with the oven door slightly open — hold it ajar with a piece of wood. Because ovens vary, check the meat after 4 or 5 hours and try a bit. When you are satisfied it is cooked and dry, store it in a plastic bag in the fridge or freezer.

You'll find it really is quite tasty, and great to take into the hills.

Chapter 23 — RECOMMENDED BOOKS

The New Zealand Outdoor Cookbook by Marcel Pilkinton

> This is a great little book containing valuable information for hunters and trampers on gear, camp cooking, food supplies and recipes. Definitely worth purchasing.

Holden's New Zealand Venison Cookbook by Philip Holden

> Available from your library. Great resource book for venison recipes.

Game for All with a flavour of Scotland by Nichola Fletcher

> An excellent book with many great game recipes — available from your library.

Creative Recipes For New Zealand Venison by Graham Brown

> For Deer Industry New Zealand contact www.nzvenison.com for a copy.

Wild and Wonderful : Everyday Venison Recipes for All Seasons by Andy Lyver

> The best book by far on venison cooking, written for New Zealand conditions.

If in doubt — ask!

ADDENDUM

Use a GPS — don't get lost.

BUTCHERS WHO SPECIALISE IN QUALITY VENISON PRODUCTS

If you have any questions don't hesitate to give any of them a call:

TAUPO FARM AND GAME MEAT PROCESSORS

15 Manuka St
Taupo
07 3788150
Contact: Bob Dailey (07 3788150)
or Andrew Elmiger (07 377 3397)

BASECAMP

504 Lockington Rd
RD2
Katikati
Bay of Plenty
Ph/Fax: 07 5520013

STOKES VALLEY QUALITY MEATS

47 Stokes Valley Road
Lower Hutt
Phone 04 5638891
Contact: Darran Meates

NB Hunters can only use a listed home kill provider to butcher their meat;

Check the following link to the NZFSA website to see if your butcher is a registered provider. www.nzfa.govt.nz/animalproducts/homekill/index.htm

II   WEBSITES OF INTEREST

Assume all websites start with www.

Most of these are New Zealand based web sites.

*Recommended (these websites deserve a good look).

If you go to my web site www.nzhuntingexp.co.nz and click on 'links', then scroll down, you will find these websites listed. Simply click on the one you want and go directly to the site. This list will be regularly updated and added to.

AMMUNITON

belmontammunition.co.nz
customcartridges.co.nz
federalcartridges.com
fusionammo.com
huntingandfishing.co.nz

ARCHERY

advancearchery.co.nz
archery.co.nz
bowandarrow.co.nz
Cabelas.com
nzap.co.nz

BUTCHERY

askthemeatman.com * (Great information for butchery)
wildnewzealand.co.nz

DVD's & VIDEOS

wildnewzealand.co.nz (Excellent DVDs on Sika, wild pigs,& butchery)

FOOD & RECIPES

adwnz.com (Food & wine)
backcountrycuisine.co.nz
nzvenison.com * (For venison recipes)
royalcuisine.co.nz/guestchef.html (More excellent venison recipes)

FIREARMS

auctionarms.com
airgun.co.nz
brownells.com * (World's largest suppliers of firearms accessories)
brownprecision.com * (Great site for lightweight rifle info)
e-gunparts.com
firearms.co.nz
gunpartshome.html
guncity.co.nz
gunindex.com
guns.co.nz
hayesandassociates.co.nz
hsprecision.com
huntingandfishing.co.nz
kiwiguns.co.nz (A New Zealand firearms auction site)

GEAR

AimTru.com
ampro.co.nz
binoculars.com
Cabelas.com
camsport.co.nz
highcountrysport.co.nz
huntech.co.nz

huntingandfishing.co.nz (Mail order)
lacklands.co.nz
legacysports.com
leupold.com
meindlboots.com
mpro7.com
nikkostirling.com
norma.cc
lymanproducts.com
outdoorsupplies.co.nz (NZ mail order)
penguindirect.co.nz
ruger.com
sako.fi
schmidtbender.com
seriousshooters.co.nz
remington.com
ridgeline.co.nz
shooters.com
stagersport.com
stoneycreek.net.nz
svord.com (Svord knives)
swazi.co.nz (Swazi clothing)
tcarms.com
tightlines.co.nz
whitetail.com
winchester.com
wileyx.co.nz

GUNSMITHS & PARTS

brownells.com * (World's largest suppliers of firearms accessories)
brownprecision.com * (Great site for lightweight rifle info)
clelandsonline.com
customcartridges.co.nz e-gunparts.com
gunsmith.co.nz
gunpartshome.html
gunworks.co.nz
mae.co.nz
rayrilingarmsbooks.com * (Numrich Arms Catalogue)

Join the
New Zealand Deerstalkers' Association
Incorporated

Fighting for Free Hunting for All

Keep deerstalking & hunting free of licence and access fees!

Important Advocacy:
- Protecting recreational hunters' interests and stopping privatisation of New Zealand's wild game and fish resource
- Working to reduce the impact of 1080 and other poisons on deer, pigs etc
- Free hunter access to recreational lands eg in South Island tenure review
- Big game - deer, tahr, chamois, pigs - recognised as valued recreational and food resources
- Supporting responsible firearms use through COLFO*

Member Services:
- The national hunters' body advocating for hunters and hunting since 1937
- HUNTS - hunter & bushcraft training programme**
- New Zealand Hunting & Wildlife magazine, Bugle Newsletter
- Liability insurance to $5 million
- 55 branches - a branch near you
- Branch rifle ranges, hunts, huts and more
- Member discounts

Hunting - a lifetime outdoor sport

COLFO* - NZ Council of Licenced Firearms Owners Incorporated
** In partnership with the NZ Mountain Safety Council. See our website: www.deerstalkers.org.nz

---

To join NZ Deerstalkers' Assn (NZDA) copy the Application Form below and send to:
NZDA, PO Box 6514, Wellington; Fax 04 801 7363; Email: office@deerstalkers.org.nz -
or apply via our website

Don't cut your magazine, just copy this info -

Yes, I want to join NZDA

Name: _ _ _ _ _ _ _ _ _ _   Tel: _ _ _ _ _ _ _

Address: _

Email: _ _ _ _ _ _ _

Under the terms of the Privacy Act 1993, I acknowledge that you are retaining my name for the purpose of mailing further information on NZDA and related matters.

The smoothest shooting rifle designed to celebrate Sako's 85th year.

SAKO 85

Model 85 Hunter
Walnut oiled stock. Silver pistol grip cap.
Safari style cheek piece.

Model 85 Hunter Laminated Stainless
Gray laminated stock. Action M only.

Model 85 Synthetic Stainless
Synthetic stock with 10 overmoulded grips.

Calibers **S** 22-250 Rem 243 Win 260 Rem 7mm-08 Rem 308 Win **SM** 270 Win Short Mag 7mm Win Short Mag 300 Win Short Mag 25-06 Rem 6.5x55 SE 270 Win **M** 7x64 30-06 Sprg 9.3x62 9.3x66 Sako Overall length **S** 1090 mm (42 7/8") **SM** 1140 mm (44 7/8") M 1100 mm (43 5/16") Barrel length **SM** 570 mm (22 7/16") **SM** 620 mm (24 3/8") Weight **S** 3.3 kg (7 1/4 lbs) **SM/M** 3.4 kg (7 1/2 lbs) Length of pull **S/SM/M** 350 mm (13 3/4") Cartridge capacity **S/M** 6 rounds (1 in chamber, 5 in magazine) **SM** 5 rounds (1 in chamber, 4 in magazine)

BERETTA
Beretta New Zealand NZ Limited PO Box 12009 Penrose

suppressor.co.nz
uhgunshop.co.nz
westerngunparts.com

HUNTING

buckpole.net
deeranddeerhunting.com
gunandgame.com
fiordland.org.nz (For Wapiti block information)
huntingandfishing.co.nz (Including second hand firearms web site)
huntingandshooting.com
nzhuntingexp.co.nz (authors web site)
sambardeer.co.nz (Sambar Foundation)

KNIVES

brentsandowknives.com
svord.com (Svord knives)

MAPS

mapworld.co.nz
memory-map.co.nz
ordernow.co.nz
polymedia.co.nz

ORGANISATIONS

BlackpowderShooters.com
colfo.org.nz
deerstalkers.org.nz (New Zealand Deerstalkers Association)
doc.govt.nz
govt.nz (A key link site for Govt)
huntingsociety.org

mountainsafety.org.nz *
nzsika.co.nz (Hunters & Habitat)
nzwt.co.nz (New Zealand Wildlife Trust)
nra.org.nz
pistolnz.org.nz
shootingnz.com
ssanz.org.nz
stop1080poison.com

RELOADING

barnesbullets.com
blackpodwder.co.nz
customcartridges.co.nz * (For reloaded ammunition)
hayesandassociates.co.nz
hodgdon.com
hodgdon.com/links/index.php * (Some great links here)
hornady.com
huntingnut.com * (Especially good for reloaders)
lymanproducts.com
nosler.com
nzammo.co.nz
reloadammo.com * (An excellent link site)
reloaders.co.nz
sierrabullets.com
6mmbr.com * (Another very useful website for reloaders)
speer-bullets.com
shooters.com

SAFETY & EMERGENCY

beacons.org.nz * (Emergency locator beacons)
mountainsafety.org.nz *
nzlsar.org.nz/sar-wx.html * (Excellent weather site plus mountain radio)

SUPPRESSORS

gunworks.co.nz
mae.co.nz (McColl Arms & Engineering)
suppressor.co.nz

TRANSPORT

airchartertaupo.co.nz
helisika.co.nz
seriousshooters.co.nz
helistar.co.nz
vulcanheli.co.nz
helipro.co.nz

TAXIDERMY

freezedrytaxidermy.co.nz
orourkebros.co.nz (taxidermy)

WEATHER

MetVUW.com
metservice.co.nz
predictweather.com
nzlsar.org.nz/sar-wx.html * (Excellent weather site plus mountain radio)

Tell someone where you are going.

III BACKCOUNTRY TRANSPORT AND CHARTER OPERATORS

NORTH ISLAND

Central North Island

Central Helicopters Ltd (Rotorua) 0800435444 www.centralheli.co.nz

Helicopters Hawkes Bay Ltd (Napier) 06 879 9242

Helihunt 'n' Fish Taupo Ltd (Taupo) 07 3842000 0274 479350 p.janssen@xtra.co.nz

Helisika (Taupo) 07 3842816 0274 543 916 helisika@xtra.co.nz www.helisika.co.nz

Lakeland Helicopters (Taupo) 07 3665267 (Murupara) 07 266 5501

Helistar Helicopters (Taupo and Turangi) 0800435478 www.helistar.co.nz

Heliwing Ltd 07 3125555 (Whakatane)

Waimana Helicopters Ltd (Whakatane) 07 312 3243 www.waiheli@wave.co.nz

East Coast

Ashworth Helicopters Ltd (Wairoa and Gisborne) 06 8677128

Gisborne Helicopters (Gisborne) 06 862 5560

Helicopters Hawkes Bay (Hastings and Waipukurau) 06 879 9242 www.helicoptershawkesbay.co.nz

Helipro Helicopters (Nationwide) 0800 435 477 www.helipro.co.nz

Outback Helicopters (Southern Hawkes Bay) 06 374 3511

Lower North Island

Amalgamated Helicopters (Wellington) 06 379 8600
www.amalgamatedheli.co.nz   amalgamatedheli@xtra.co.nz

Helipro Helicopters (Nationwide) 0800 435 477
www.helipro.co.nz

Heli-Flight Ltd (Wellington) 0800 768 6771
www.heliflight.co.nz   info@heliflight.co.nz

Hill Country Helicopters Ltd (Wanganui and Taihape) 06 343 1843
marktilyard@hotmail.co.nz

Rangitikei Helicopters Ltd (Rangitikei) 06 328 6887

Wanganui Aero-Work (Taihape and Raetihi) 0800 492 642
www.aerowork.co.nz   operations@aerowork.co.nz

SOUTH ISLAND

Nelson

Coast to Coast Helicopters Ltd (Mapua) 03 540 2546

Nelson Helicopters Ltd (Nelson) 0800 450 350
www.nelsonhelicopters.co.nz   enquiries@nelsonhelicopters.co.nz

Tasman Helicopters (Motueka) 03 528 8075
www.tasmanhelicopters.co.nz

Canterbury

Alpine Springs Helicopters (Christchurch) 03 315 7165

Amuri Helicopters (Hamner Springs) 0800 888 308

Christchurch Helicopters (Christchurch) 03 359 0470
info@chchheli.co.nz

Garden City Helicopters (Christchurch) 03 358 4360
www.helicopters.net.nz

Helipro Helicopters (Christchurch) 0800435 477   www.helipro.co.nz

Mt Hutt Helicopters (Christchurch) 0800 443 547
www.mthuttheli.co.nz   info@mthuttheli.co.nz

West Coast

Auhaura Helicopters Ltd (Grey Valley) 03 732 3668
AuhauraHelicopters@xtra.co.nz

Airwest Helicopters Ltd (Reefton) 0800 532 888

Alpine Adventures (Fox Glacier) 0800 800 0866
Fox_heli@xtra.co.nz

Coastwide Helicopters Ltd (Greymouth) 03 762 6117
coastwide@xtra.co.nz

Glacier Heliventures (Franz Joseph) 03 752 0688

Helicopter Charter Karamea (Karamea) 03 782 6111

Heliventures Ltd (Haast) 0800 750 086
www.heliventures.co.nz

Kokatahi Helicopters 2000 Ltd (Hokitika) 03 755 7912

www.kokatahihelicopters.co.nz

Mountain Helicopters (Fox Glacier) 0800 369 423
www.mountainhelicopters.co.nz

The Helicopter Line (Franz Joseph) 0800 807 767
www.helicopter.co.nz   mjglynn@xtra.co.nz

Otago

Aspiring Helicopters (Wanaka) 03 443 7152

Back Country Helicopters (Hawea) 03 4431054   027 212 6957
www.backcountryhelicopters.com

Heliworks (Queenstown) 0508 249 7167
www.southernlakeshelicopters.co.nz

Nokomai Helicopters 027 286 5141

Nordic Helicopters (Queenstown) 0800 667 342
www.nordichelicopters.co.nz

Southland

Air Milford 03 442 2351

Foveaux Helicopters (Invercargill) 03 214 1514
www.foveauxhelicopters.co.nz

Fiordland Helicopters (Te Anau) 03 249 7575
www.fiordlandhelicopters.co.nz

Heliworks (Te Anau & Invercargill) 0508 249 7167 (Toll Free)
www.heliworks.co.nz

Helisouth Ltd (Invercargill) 0800 435 476 ww.helisouth.co.nz

Herbie & Lorraine Hansen (Stewart Island) charter boat 03 2101133
ilhansen@xtra.co.nz

Mana Charters (Bluff) 03 212 7254
www.manacharters.com

Milford Helicopters 03 2498384 (Te Anau)
milford.helicopters@xtra.co.nz

Mount Anglem Helicopters (Bluff) 03 2127700
www.mtanglemhelicopters.co.nz

Rakiura Helicopters (Stewart Island) 03 2191155 0272219217
www.rakiurahelicopters.co.nz

Southern Lakes Helicopters Ltd (Invercargill and Te Anau) 0508 249 7167
www.southernlakeshelicopters.co.nz
info@southernlakeshelicopters.co.nz

South West Helicopters (Invercargill, Tuatapere and Te Anau) 0800 435 476
www.southwesthelicopters.co.nz   info@southwesthelicopters.co.nz

Southland Air Services (Invercargill) 03 21 1310 021 701 672
sthtravl@southnet.co.nz

IV TAXIDERMISTS

Graeme Wood

PO Box 65
Waipu
Northland
Ph 09 432 0886
025 276 26667

Big Game Artistry

Mark Walker
386 Ngahinapouri Road
RD 2
Ohaupo
mwalker@actrix.co.nz
Ph 07 825 2105

Sika Country Taxidermy Ltd

Vern Pearson and Louise Birksø
Sika Country Taxidermy
980 Poihipi Road
R.D. 1
Taupo
sikacountry@hotmail.com
Ph/fax 07 378 4908

Wildlife Art Ltd

Peter and Karina Livesey
198 Palmer Mill Road
Taupo
Ph 07 377 3063
Fax 07 377 1505
karinapete@xtra.co.nz

Peter Wells

Wildlife Arts and Taxidermy
PO Box 1240
Rotorua
taxidermy@xtra.co.nz
Ph 07 345 3650
027 4143657

Steve Barclay

PO Box 36
Mangaweka
Ph 06 382 5787
021 171 2117
steven_barclay@msn.com

Kaweka Taxidermy

Wayne and Crystal McPhedran
Waipukarau
Ph 06 878 3438
025 248 2847

Freeze Dry Taxidermy

Richard Lee
779 Makuri Road
Stratford
Ph 06 762 7955
025 450 249

The Taxidermy Shop

Craig Ferguson
Cliff Road
RD 1 Marton thetaxidermyshop@telstra.net.nz
Ph 06 327 5438

David Jacobs

PO Box 4058
Christchurch
tjacobs@clear.net.nz
Ph 03 338 4266

Mosgiel Taxidermy Studio

Gary Pullar
46 Snowdon Street
RD 2
Allantown
Mosgiel
Ph 03 489 4494

Tyron Southward Taxidermy Ltd

10 Railway Road
Dunsandal
Canterbury
Ph/Fax 03 325 4545

O'Rourke Brothers

85 Main Road
Pleasant Point
South Canterbury
Ph 03 614 7737

GUNSMITHS

Allen J Carr

10 Hurley Rd
Paraparaumu Beach
Kapiti Coast
Wellington
Ph/Fax: 04 905 0847
Mob: 021 234 6115

Custom Cartridges

38 B Arthur Crescent
Taupo
Ph: 07 3784593
Email: mark@nzsika.co.nz
www.customcartridges.co.nz

D.F Maisey

PO Box 14 006
Tauranga
Ph/Fax: 07 544 2207
Email: dean@gunsmith.co.nz
Web:www.gunsmith.co.nz

D W Collings and Bradey

104 Campbell St
Karori
Wellington
Ph: 04 476 8460
Fax: 04 476 4778

High Country Sports

Fairlie 8771
South Canterbury
Ph: 03 6858906
Web: wwwhighcountrysport.co.nz

John Hall Gunsmith

Wilson Road
South Head
Helensville
Ph: 09 420 2837
Email:trujon@xtra.co.nz

Keith Frazier Gunsmith

PO Box 2234
Tauranga
Ph: 07 573 6640
Mob: 025 2477029

McColl Arms and Engineering

1a/64 Ellice Rd
Glenfield
Auckland
Ph: 09 414 1142
Mob: 021 639 667
Email: m.a.e@xtra.co.nz
Web: www. suppressor.co.nz
Web: www.mae.co.nz

Precision Arms Hunting and Fishing

171 Main St
Otautau
Southland
Ph/Fax: 03 225 8232

Mob: 021 148 3818
Email:precisionarms@hotmail.com

Robert Dollimore

588 Spencer Rd
Lake Tarawera
Rotorua
Ph/Fax: 07 362 8447

Shane Longney

RD9
Te Puke
Ph/Fax: 07 533 2212

Upper Hutt Gun Shop

29a Montgomery Crescent
Upper Hutt
Ph: 04 939 6184
Fax: 04 939 4798
Email:uhgunshop@paradise.net.nz
Web:www.uhgunshop.co.nz

Campbell and Webster Gunshop

PO Box 195
Waiuku
Auckland
Ph: 09 534 7517
Mob: 025 837 072

A WARNING

A key issue at present facing firearms owners is VOLUNTARY REGISTRATION. Please note you are NOT required by law to register your firearms. However, when firearms owners are required to re-licence, the vetters, or representatives of the police, ask them to <u>voluntarily</u> register their firearms. This may seem an innocuous thing to do, but you need to note several things here:

1. Not all licence vetters at the re- registration interviews tell the firearms owner that they have a choice as to whether they register their firearms or not. Draw your own conclusions.

2. Details of your firearms are recorded on the police computer.

3. If you refuse to register your firearms this refusal is recorded on your file, in my opinion as a black mark and may be used against you later on—otherwise why do they record it? I know this is the case in the UK where they are much further down the track in outlawing all private firearms ownership.

4. While we are assured that the motives of the Police re registration are to give another record for the owner, they cannot assure us that a future government bent on outlawing private ownership of firearms will not use this information to confiscate our firearms. Knowledge is power and I prefer to give the Police and Government as little potential power over me as possible. Remember the Arms Officers or vetters do not make policy, they implement it.

In my opinion this move by the Police re voluntary registration is "registration by stealth" and should be resisted at every turn. In virtually every country where there has been registration, it has been followed by confiscation! Do you want your firearms confiscated in the future? My advice is this: when you are asked to register your firearms, politely say "No, thank you!"

What you need to do is:

i. Make sure you have more than adequate security for your firearms. You must keep your firearms in a secure place, safe from children and opportunist burglars.

ii. Keep your own record of what firearms you own and their identification numbers in a separate and secure place.

iii. Record details of who you sell your firearms to if you sell them privately i.e. record the purchaser's Firearms Licence number.

iv. Make it an <u>absolute priority</u> to belong to a hunting organisation or shooting club so we can have strength in working together to protect our rights and our future. Below is list of various hunting and shooting organisations you may like to consider. Look on their websites or give them a call, but don't be a lone voice or a hunter "doing your own thing!"

New Zealand Hunting and Shooting Organisations.

- New Zealand Deerstalkers' Association
  Phone: 04 8017367
  Email: office@deerstalkers.org.nz
  Website: www.deerstalkers.org.nz

- Hunters and Habitat
  Phone: 07 3784593
  Email: mark@nzsika.co.nz
  Website: www.nzsika.co.nz

- Safari Club International
  Phone: 03 3436339
  Email: SCINZ@xtra.co.nz
  Website: www.scinz.com

- Game and Forest Foundation
  Phone: 04 3850097
  Email: info@gameandforest.co.nz
  Website: www.gameandforest.co.nz

- Sporting Shooters Association
  Phone: 09 8321724

- COLFO — Council of Licensed Firearms Owners Inc
  Phone: 027 6719385

Email: info@colfo.org.nz
Website: www.colfo.org.nz

- NZ Pistol Association Inc
  Phone: 04 2377500
  Email: info@pistolnz.org.nz
  Website: www.pistolnz.org.nz

- NRA –National Rifle Association
  Phone: 04 5284843

- Frontier and Western Shooting Sports Assn
  Phone: 06 3796692

- Auckland Rifle Association
  Phone: 09 8188224
  Email: Bruce.Millard@xtra.co.nz

- IMAS — International Military Arms Society Incorporated
  Email: bigal@siliconlogic.co.nz
  Website: www.imas.co.nz

- New Zealand Service Rifle Association
  Email: NZSRA@xtra.co.nz

- NZ Black Powder Shooters Association
  Phone: 07 3460470
  Email: powdermonkey@paradise.net.nz

- Wellington Service Rifle Association
  Phone: 04 3801681
  Website: servicerifle.forum.org.nz

- NZAAA — NZ Antique and Historical Arms Assn Inc
  Email: info@nzaa.org.nz
  Website: www.antiquearms.org.mz

- New Zealand Bowhunters Society
  Phone (07) 5432577
  Email: nzbowhunters@hotmail.com

VII REVIEW OF NON-COMMERCIAL WILD FOOD IN NEW ZEALAND

Excerpts from:

Report to New Zealand Food Safety Authority from the Institute of Environmental Science and Research Ltd by Nicola Turner, Peter Cressey, Dr Rob Lake and Rosemary Whyte.

(NB: This booklet contains valuable information and is most worthwhile reading for anyone who harvests wild food in New Zealand. I'm grateful to the New Zealand Food Safety Authority for permission to use this material — Author)

A copy of the full report is available from:

New Zealand Food Safety Authority
P O Box 2835
WELLINGTON
Telephone : (04) 463 2500
Fax : (04) 463 2501

Website
A copy of this document can be found at www.nzfa.govt.nz

Feral Land Animals

4:1 Introduction

Deer are the main big game harvested by non-commercial hunters, but goats, pigs, wallabies, rabbits, hares and possums are all important target species. For all of these animals the number harvested non-commercially for food, as opposed to sport or pest control, is difficult to determine. Under the Animal Products Act, non-commercial hunters and hunting are not regulated.

4:2 Food Description: Feral Land Animals

4:2:1 Feral deer

Approximately 250,000 deer, made up from seven species, are distributed throughout the forests, scrublands and grasslands of New Zealand, consuming grasses, herbs and foliage of forest trees and shrubs (Coleman and Cooke, 2001; DOC, 2002). The Red deer (Cervus ealphus; tia) is the most numerous and widespread, with deer densities estimated at 2–5 per km^2 in the South Island and 5–15 per km^2 in the North Island (Lindsey and Morris, 2000; Eason, 2002a). Fallow deer (Dama dama) and Sika deer (Cervus nippon) are also abundant (Coleman and Cooke, 2001). Wapiti deer (Cervus canadensis), Sambar deer (Cervus unicolor), Rusa deer (Cervus timorensis) and White-tailed deer (Odocoileus virginianus) are all confined to only a few locations in New Zealand and have comparatively small populations (DOC, 2002).

4:3 Data for Exposure Assessment: Feral Land Animals

Please refer to the "Points for consideration" in Section 1.5.

The NZFSA Animal Products Group administers a chemical residue monitoring programme under which samples from farmed and feral animals submitted for slaughter and registered premises are randomly tested for a variety of agricultural compounds and other chemicals. Some results from this programme are included in the following sections, and were kindly supplied by the Animal Products Group (NZFSA) or sourced from annual report issues of Surveillance.

4:3:1 Deer

Hazard prevalence

Heavy metals

Of 62 kidney samples from feral deer commercially slaughtered in 1988/99, the level of cadmium in around 50% was below 0.49 mg/kg. Approximately 15% were between 1.00 and 1.99 mg/kg, and 5% exceeded 2.00 mg/kg. The cadmium was likely to have been consumed and retained from naturally occurring sources in the environment. As cadmium bioaccumulates in the kidney, older animals had higher levels than younger due to longer exposure. This could be problematic for hunters who target older deer (Roberts et al., 1994).

Chemical control agents

The livers from several feral animal species are tested for the presence of brodifacoum, pindone and flocoumafen under the NZFSA chemical residue monitoring programme (pindone monitoring was discontinued in 2001/2002). All feral deer tested between 1999 and 2004 were negative for brodifacoum, pindone and flocoumafen residues. The feral deer sampled included 475 Red deer, 11 Fallow deer, 3 Sika deer, 2 Rusa deer and 1 Sambar deer.

Brodifacoum residues were tested for in 26 deer shot from areas where brodifacoum bait was in use for possum and rodent control. Residues were detected in the livers of 39% of the samples at concentrations ranging from 0.01 to 0.03 mg/kg. Of 15 feral deer shot from areas where brodifacoum baiting had ceased at least six months previously, none showed any residue. One deer muscle sample had a brodifacoum residue of 0.02 mg/kg but no liver sample was collected from this animal (Eason et al., 2001).

Muscle samples from feral deer were tested for 1080 residues under the NZFSA chemical residue monitoring programme between 1999 and 2004. Two positive samples were reported in 1999 out of a total over the five years of 343 Red deer, 9 Fallow deer, 3 Sika deer, 2 Rusa deer and 1 Sambar deer. One of the positive samples was suspected to have been caused by contamination in the transport vehicle taking the animal to the processor. There was no obvious source of the 1080 residues in the second positive sample, as the animal had been shot in an area where 1080 had not been laid.

Feral deer can be killed by 1080 during poisoning programmes and the LD_{50} is 0.5 mg/kg (Eason, 2002a). It has been estimated that 5–54% of Red deer and 66–75% of Fallow deer are killed during aerial 1080 poisoning operations using cereal bait or carrots. There are no data on 1080 residues in sub-lethally exposed deer, but it is likely to be low and short-term.

Environmental contaminants

The low water solubility and tendency for DDT to adsorb onto solids makes it very persistent in the soil. The ingestion of topsoil by herbivores causes low-level residues in body fat (Harrison, 1971). No data were found on the residues of DDT or other organochlorine pesticides in feral deer.

Bacterial pathogens

Clinical leptospirosis has been recognised in feral deer but little is known about the prevalence (Reichel et al., 1999). The serovars hordjo, pomona, and copenhageni have all been reported in farmed deer and some studies suggest that the prevalence of asymptomatic infection is high in these populations, while others have found a low prevalence (Wilson et al., 1998; Reichel et al., 1999; Wilson, 2002a). The disparities may arise from regional differences in the prevalence of infection, which could potentially occur in feral populations (Reichel et al., 1999).

Other than a few sporadic cases in domestic stock, Listeria infection is uncommon in New Zealand farmed deer (Staples, 1997). The infection rate in feral deer is not known.

Mycobacterium bovis is present in feral deer. It requires constant input from an external source such as possums, but deer possibly amplify the frequency of infection in certain areas, as they are capable of infecting livestock or other wild animals. Deer are most likely infected through the oral route by inhalation or ingestion, particularly through contact with ill or dying possums. Deer-to-deer transmission appears to be infrequent, although this may depend on population density. The prevalence of M. bovis infection is high in some deer populations, particularly in the Wairarapa, Central North Island and West Coast. Most reports of TB relate to Red deer, though the disease has been found in other deer species. Out of 106 wild Red deer from TB endemic areas, 32% were confirmed by culture as being infected. The prevalence of infection in endemic areas from other studies was 18% and 27%. Prevalence as high as 37% has been reported. The prevalence in non-endemic areas (no infection in possums) have been reported as 2.0% and 0.8%. It has been suggested that around one-quarter of infected deer show no detectable lesions indicating the presence of M. bovis, and infected carcasses may enter the food chain. M. bovis has also been isolated from Sika and Fallow deer at low frequency (Lugton et al., 1998; Coleman and Cooke, 2001; Nugent et al., 2001).

There are no data on the prevalence of Salmonella infection in feral deer populations. The pathogen has been isolated rarely from clinically ill farmed deer, but not from 3,810 faecal samples from healthy deer (Wilson, 2002b).

There are no data on the prevalence of yersiniosis in feral deer populations, but the disease is common in farmed deer, so could potentially be present in wild populations. Of 153 farmed deer (varied species) found dead or close to death, 19% were mortally infected with yersiniosis, making this the most common infectious cause of death in the sample. The species of Yersinia causing infection was Y. pseudotuberculosis, which is rarely transmitted to humans but has been associated with liver disease (Jawetz et al., 1978). Yersiniosis was more common in the cooler months (June to November) and younger age classes were more affected (Jerrett et al., 1990).

Viral pathogens

No data found.

Parasitic pathogens

Sarcocystis spp. have been found in 30% (n=50) of red deer from Rotorua (Collins and Charleston, 1979), but the source of the deer was not clear. The prevalence of Toxoplasma gondii infection in feral deer is not known. It has been estimated that the overall proportion of farmed deer seropositive for Toxoplasma is 52.5% (Reichel et al., 1999). Deer are susceptible to liver fluke infection (P. Mason, pers. comm.).

Harvesting and consumption

A few estimates have been made on the number of deer harvested non-commercially in New Zealand. From a survey conducted in 1992/93 and the number of permits issued nationally, Fraser (2000) estimated a national harvest of 17,905 Red deer and 39,830 deer belonging to other species. In a later survey, Nugent (1992) estimated that 41,662 Red deer were hunted from the ground annually. Estimates were also made for the annual ground-based hunting of Sika deer (6,845), Fallow deer (3,921), and deer of other species (1,833) (Nugent, 1992). Of these, 16.2% were sold as carcasses. For comparison, hunting for commercial purposes has been estimated at an annual rate of 10,000–30,000 deer (Parkes and Murphy, 2003), or more specifically, 17,173 red deer and 5,503 other deer species (Nugent, 1992). In all cases Red deer were the most common quarry and were hunted by 86% of deer hunters.

Most deer are taken by stalking on foot, either alone, in groups, or with a pointing dog. A small number are taken with the aid of spotlights or in traps, and helicopter hunting is popular in some areas. Most hunting is conducted on public land, and the rest from private farmland (around a third) (Nugent, 1992; Fraser, 2000). Hunting occurs year-round, though mostly in weekends, and there is more emphasis on stag hunting during the rut. Larger animals are favoured when herds are encountered (Lentle et al., 2000).

Potentially all fleshy parts of the deer can be eaten either as cuts or when made into meat products (e.g. sausages). Venison is usually eaten cooked. Venison was reported to be consumed by 0.4% of respondents in the 1997 National Nutrition Survey, with an average serving size for those consuming of 165g. Overall this equates to a mean daily intake of venison of 0.6 g/person/day for the total population (Russell et al., 1999). The NNS data gave no indication of the source of the venison, and it is likely that deer harvesters will consume a much higher amount than this average intake.

The consuming population

Non-commercial wild animal hunting is dominated by males — 7% of male New Zealanders rated hunting and shooting as one of their favourite leisure activities. All age classes participate though there are fewer men above 45 years of age. Rural people are more likely to be involved in hunting than urban dwellers. A 1988 survey found that there were around 50,000 active big-game hunters, including around 40,000 deer hunters. The motivation is to obtain trophies, venison, or both, or to enjoy the outdoors (Fraser, 2000). There is no strong ethnic trend.

Hunters must have a permit. Approximately 63,500 permits are issued annually for recreational hunting throughout New Zealand, with the number issued depending on the issue system in each region, the deer species present and area available to hunt in (Fraser, 2000).

Venison is commonly shared with family and friends.

VIII   FINAL COMMENTS

Hunting is a fantastic sport. There's nothing quite like the freshness of an awakening dawn, dew heavy on the ground, and early golden rays of the sun seeking to penetrate the morning gloom as you expectantly begin your stalk down the flats or towards a clearing. Then the shrill sound of a Sika stag in full cry pierces the dawn from deep in the dark bush and your heart leaps in anticipation.

Who knows what the day will bring forth? Maybe this is the day you'll get the big one! Or maybe this is one day he will win the uneven contest and you will tell your mates about the huge stag you almost shot, vowing "next time"! And it's that next time that calls you out again and again and again.

Yes, hunting is a fantastic sport — heart-breaking challenges and lifelong relationships forged in trying conditions, God's creation at its inspiring best, fresh clean fun devoid of PC idiocy and bureaucratic nonsense, where the true realities of life are seen reflected in the rainbow, the storm, the bush, the rivers and the awe-inspiring mountains.

Enjoy it, hunt with an eye to the future and look beyond yourself. It's not what you take that ultimately matters; it's what you become and what you give.

Safe and successful hunting.

Alex Gale